THE DYING UTOPIA

«La chimère du jour est d'enrichir toutes les classes aux dépens les unes des autres; c'est de généraliser la Spoliation sous prétexte de l'organiser.»

– Frédéric Bastiat

TABLE OF CONTENTS

1. THE DISINFORMATION SOCIETY — 4

2. INTERNATIONAL SOCIALISM — 14

3. NATIONAL SOCIALISM — 30

4. SOCIAL DEMOCRATISM — 49

5. LAW AS INSTRUMENTUM REGNI — 81

6. TAXATION: THE ROAD TO REDISTRIBUTION — 100

7. ECONOMICS VERSUS SOCIALISM — 126

8. DEBT AND SPENDING — 148

9. PROBLEMS AND SOLUTIONS — 164

REFERENCE LIST — 193

1. THE DISINFORMATION SOCIETY

This book is not intended to be a particularly complete treatise. Rather, it is intended to give the reader a rough overview of the truly essential and important issues that concern all persons of First World countries in the next few decades. The book serves to educate the reader about the historical preclusion of social democracy and its later worldwide primacy in the twentieth century—at least in the First World countries. The underlying ideological core must be properly examined and contrasted with the other forms of socialism. The author suggests that the system of social democracy is unfit for the fast-paced world of the twenty-first century and will especially not survive the change from an economy based primarily on people in the service sector to one that is based on artificial superintelligence, computing, and robotics.

Politically left people live, think, and argue using socialist emotion, compared to those grounded in politically right liberal rationalism. All attempts at debating any issues must therefore fail, since both sides will never be able to come to terms with the same axioms and therefore base their argumentation on entirely different assumptions. The liberal thinks that humans are inherently capable of acting for and in their best interest at all times. Socialists think that humans are inherently incapable of acting for and in their best interest at all times. This is why they favor large, collective groups, legislation, and redistribution. These measures, by enlightened leaders, are supposed to help compensate for the defects of the human. The result of socialism is the predictable degeneration of individuality and, therefore, the loss of unpredictable human action. The liberal, on the other hand, believes that only as an individual can he reach his true potential. He can use other individuals as a way to achieve his own goals. By achieving his own goals, he always helps others achieve theirs. The result of liberalism is unpredictable human action, always for the benefit of oneself, which, in turn, benefits everyone since all individuals use each other to achieve their own means.

To prime the reader, this chapter serves to show that many special interest groups uphold social democracy through media and other organizations. The seemingly conflicting interests and allegedly opposed nature of the so-called mainstream and alternative media are not conflicting if one understands the stakes involved in the ideology of social democratism. What might understandably appear bizarre to the mean reader is an important prerequisite for understanding why those known pertinent media outlets, non-governmental organizations, and government agencies all adhere to at least low-level manipulation and framing to uphold a generally positive image of social democracy. What have they to gain? Non-governmental organizations have a great deal of influence on the political policies of today[1]. They possess the ability to form the opinions of the general mass of people on a scale previously not thought possible. The ever-changing forms of mass media, from magazines, newspapers, and pamphlets in the nineteenth century, over radio, television, and the internet in the twentieth century, to social media of the twenty-first century, all have helped perpetuate these preformed opinions. The main strategy of most multinational non-governmental organizations today, no matter the political label, is to work together with government agencies and other organizations to preserve the status quo and protect the primacy of social democratism.

One might ask why organizations that appear to compete with each other would unite to prevent the downfall of social democratism. The answer lies in the ideology itself. It is a moderate form of socialism. The recent historical struggle in the nineteenth and twentieth centuries between extreme forms of international and national forms of socialism has led many people with high stakes in the economy to attempt to stabilize this system, which promises compromises between the two systems of liberalism and socialism. It does not require much forethought to realize that

---

1   *van der Reijden* (2005/2023) provides an extensive list.

liberalism and socialism counteract each other. The alternative to this system might not be liberalism, though. As history has shown, the slow transition from liberalism to socialism in the past two hundred years is hard to ignore—whether that is political or economic. The underlying cause of this shift in the mentality of entire groups of people is primarily to blame on the mean population. Most of those people are ignorant and uneducated, especially in economic and financial matters.

It appears the fundamentals of social democratic ideas have been «[...] *established as a conventional judgment, unquestionably accepted and agreed to by everybody [...]*[2]» albeit most proponents of social democracies are unwilling to follow through with the extreme socialist ideology. The reader will find that international socialist agitators ran into similar issues as the growing working population after the Industrial Revolution grew wealthier and accumulated more stakes in the economic system of the nineteenth century. Similarly, the average person in the modern social democracy has large stakes, in an economic sense but more so in the form of claims against the welfare state. Such a concept was still entirely alien to the nineteenth-century person. As such, even those with poor financial literacy must realize the detrimental effect that a revolution could potentially have on their economic status in the population. The

---

2   *Bastiat/Cain (transl.)/de Huszar (ed.) (1995), 272.*

mere chance of such a revolution occurring is enough to alienate them from such extreme socialist ideologies. Contrasting this behavior to times of relative economic distress, such as the 1920s and early 1930s in Germany, which led to the national socialists assuming power, one finds that people in economic distress are more likely to pursue radical reforms. Another example of this phenomenon is the New Deal of the United States, during and after the great economic correction of the 1930s. The wealthier people become, due to rapidly increasing technology and productivity, the less likely it is for them to commit to extreme socialist ideologies. They become more likely to constantly favor compromises to increase their chances of protecting their standing in the economy against the potential threat of an extreme socialist revolution. Favoring compromises often leads to them slowly being expropriated anyway, which seems to be of secondary concern to them. They would much rather praise social democracy for allegedly being wholly responsible for allowing them to have a relatively high standard of living.

The goal of mainstream media coverage is to ensure a mostly positive view of social democratism. Therefore, most minor issues plaguing social democracies today are usually brushed off completely. On the other hand, the alternative media usually blows them out of proportion. The reader will soon understand why this must occur. The real issues are not being addressed properly, with the same vigor, by either form of mass media. Discourse between truly differing opinions is missing. Instead, the mainstream and alternative media must constantly insult each other and question the other party's intelligence. This appears strange, simply because it is forced behavior. By having an institution of alternative media that constantly clashes with the ‹mainstream› opinion, social democratic states can easily purport the illusion of discourse and alternative opinion. If the mainstream and alternative media were truly genuine, they could easily ignore each other's antics. The collective harmony in any given social democracy must always come before problem-solving. After all, calm sheep herds are easier to deal with than those frigthened by the big, bad wolf. Since the mass media today, whether mainstream or alternative, is the main medium of interaction with allowable opinions nowadays, there exist specific tactics that are being incorporated to indoctrinate people within the different iterations of allowable political dogma.

Before a topic is denied by officials or riddled with misinformation by mainstream media, the easiest option to slow down discourse is to ignore it. If a situation is not acknowledged by the mainstream media at all, most people will forget about the topic soon when they feel that it is insignificant enough. Typically, one can see that topics that are being reported on in alternative media are ignored in mainstream media; the same happens inversely as well. Especially when people are bombarded with other irrelevant information in the modern environment of information overload, focusing on key issues is hard for the mean person. Avoiding the main problem and only talking about unimportant side issues can be sufficient to stop serious discussions about an important issue. The more complex a topic, the easier it is for the average person to dismiss it as too complicated to waste time on. Those people would much rather choose the comfortable option of letting experts solve the issue for them. The stronger version of misinformation is disinformation. Unlike misinformation that tries to disguise the gravity of a topic or cover it up, disinformation encourages discussion about the topic while knowingly forming the opinion in the discussions around artificially fabricated disinformation.

This can typically be spotted around topics that seemingly have an endless supply of multiple conflicting theories. Disinformation is usually implemented when a topic becomes too large or convoluted to ignore or too important for confusion to be successful on larger scales. The main role of the controlled opposition ‹alternative media› is to spread such disinformation. Although mainstream media is much more adherent to misinformation and framing, the alternative media, because of its overwhelming controlled opposition nature, is disproportionately loaded with disinformation. Most topics allowed for discussion are those of a controlled opposition nature, whose discussion benefits no one. All topics discussed in alternative media have a veil of speculation and mystery surrounding them to hide the lack of truth. Usually, in a disinformation campaign, it is ensured that the theories conflict with each other as much as possible. That way, most people will not be able to reach a sound conclusion about the given topic without digging deep enough to realize that all the presented opinions are false. Checking every statement, opinion, and fact, regardless of source, is imperative for becoming aware of disinformation, some of which is quite sophisticated nowadays.

The internet has acted as a catalyst for disinformation because any kind of information can now travel both faster and further, in a shorter time, than in previous decades and centuries. The amount of information has increased drastically as well, meaning that the mean population is more dependent on some form of media than ever. On a more positive note, the internet has led to many disinformation techniques becoming ineffective because much of today's information is freely accessible and verifiable. On the other hand, emerging artificial general intelligence opens up entirely new ways of using disinformation to one's advantage, some of which are hard to notice without deep research. Even framing can have serious effects on the population. In the consensus of allowable opinion, the mainstream media and various organizations have played a major role over the last few decades, especially in North America, in creating a stereotype of the drug-consuming, violent, rapping, hoodlum african-american, with poor speech patterns. This is quite similar to the behavior of low-income white people in the southern states of the United States, who originally came from poor parts of Great Britain in previous centuries[3]. Because today african-americans are being encouraged to conform to those stereotypes, as a result, many young african-americans are discouraged from pursuing worthwhile careers, some of them being unable to stay away from thrift, while others suffer from self-victimization, and others glorify gangs and prison life. It certainly does not help that the music industry and other organizations capitalized on this phenomenon by alleging that this is ‹true black culture›, that must be celebrated and preserved. This act of framing alienates qualified african-american people while celebrating unqualified black people. The easily conditionable part of society is vulnerable to both sides of media populism because it gives them comfort when people perpetuate their worldview. The two forms of media balance themselves out. Any form of media is a perfect tool for creating a false consensus among a broad population. Similar programming each day conditions people into reinforcing certain opinions.

In that regard, the mass media makes their viewers docile while slightly agitating or nudging them towards certain opinions. On the side of alternative media,

---

3   *Sowell* (2005), 28.

especially big radio shows and podcasts that specialize in conspiracy theories, aliens, or new-age thinking, are key offenders. The alternative media suffers from grand amounts of disinformation by controlled opposition, such as denying that planes flew into the Pentagon, flat earthers, new-age religion, no moon landing theories, everything being controlled by Freemasons and the Illuminati, reptilians, anti-usury, and many more concerning theories that everyone with basic knowledge about the given topic will be able to disprove easily. The controlled opposition ties of prominent figures in alternative media circles become visible if one can think clearly without ideology getting in the way. The author is absolutely sure that most large alternative media outlets have controlled opposition assets in their lines due to the shallowness of the argumentation, often leading to nothing but more speculation.

In the following three chapters, the different forms of socialism will be evaluated and contrasted. This is imperative to understand social democracy in its current form. Afterwards, the role of legislation and taxation is examined. Furthermore, established economic principles will be described, and the social-democratic divergence will be illustrated. To conclude the book, the major challenges of the first half of this century are quickly introduced, and an alternative system to social democracy is presented to the reader. Each chapter concludes with a short summary.

2. INTERNATIONAL SOCIALISM

The foundation of the socialist mind is the collective and the idea of being liberated from oppression. This is to be contrasted with the idea of liberty, as found in liberalism. One author proclaims that socialism discovers facts of nature in social institutions and then tries to change nature by reforming the institutions[4]. This is problematic because social institutions only exist because of nature. They should not conform nature to themselves. Another author suggests that socialism is legal plunder[5]. This sets socialism apart from liberalism —an ideology whose proponents strive to protect from plunder precisely through legal measures. The commonly used and false definition of a liberal, used mostly in North America, refers to a socialist-inclined person. As such, the term liberalism in this book is used in the correct and historical sense, describing what is today referred to as classical liberalism. Because socialism, no matter its form, embraces the collective, the individual under socialism is merely a fragment of said collective. This does not necessarily have to be an economic collective, as seen under the Mao dictatorship in communist China. It can also assume an intellectual

---

4 *von Mises* (1951/2012), 101.
5 *Bastiat/Sterling (transl.)* (1850/1891), 18.

form and incorporate relative unanimity on certain topics. As the collective is the most important unit of measurement, under socialism, the state must rid its subordinates of everything compromising the greater good of the collective. The greater good encompasses the subjective interests of the state and all its potential subordinates in a collectivized form. The fact that this term is not properly defined does create serious problems when the state tries to rid its citizens of certain mental dispositions that are seen as harmful to the welfare of the collective. For that reason, socialism discourages individual difference out of safety, since different opinions, cultures, societal differences, and more could create fragmentation within the collective, leading to a perceived lesser form of harmony.

This, in turn, disrupts the egalitarian worldview. All differences in lifestyle, culture, and history that potentially took centuries and millennia to form may erode sooner than later. The socialist fosters hate and resentment towards the individual who dares to speak out or be different, to ensure that people want to identify with the collective out of fear of being ostracized, at the very least. To uphold the view of egalitarianism, the socialist state has to create certain aspects that the population can unite over. The most common design of such a system includes the roles of the oppressor and the oppressed. The oppressor role is imperative for the victim because, without it, no victim exists. This role has historically been filled with ‹capitalists›, Jews, Christians, fascists, racists, etc. The alleged victim is usually a uniform group that is being somehow oppressed by the oppressor. In the case of socialism, the oppressor is hallucinated by the victim. It is obvious that socialism is not limited to its historical understanding of working class versus property owner. There are many forms of socialism—class-based, race-based, gender-based, or religion-based socialism, to name a few. Although the goal of collectivism is harmony and equality, utopian socialist concepts, such as the phalanstère of *Charles Fourier*, give insight into the unrealistic image of humanity that socialists have taken inspiration from over the centuries. The phalanstère was a socialist idea of a monastery-like, self-sufficient community in which harmony was to be achieved through cooperation, redistribution of goods and property, and free love.

All extreme forms of socialism necessitate totalitarianism to bridge the gap between government and daily life and create an all-encompassing state. Social democratism, as a moderate form of socialism, is the exception to this rule. Because socialist states will never receive full support from their citizens, they put in much effort to recruit and indoctrinate children, since those are still moldable and plastic enough. The centralized schooling ensures that the children are aligned with government-mandated values. This thought pattern can be observed in most socialist ideas of ideal schooling, whether in theory or practice. In the theoretical conceptions of socialism, school always plays an important role. Even in practice, not only the Soviet Union, the Third Reich, and the People's Republic of China have indoctrinated children in school and childhood. Current governments in social democracies do the same, albeit more subduedly, through *political education,* which is supposed to teach the alleged positive values of social democracy while remaining relatively uncritical of all the inherent defects.

Socialism is an ideology of forced, artificial evolution. Old morals, traditions, and cultural values must be purged for the new human to survive and thrive, which is why death tolls in the millions were easily dismissed as necessary. In countries under socialist regimes, even former ones, the morals of the majority of the population are irreparably corrupted, as evident by the disproportionately high amount of corruption under many former communist governments. It is important to note that no singular event has caused more suffering and killed more people than the state has directly and indirectly, through its policies and wars. Socialism is truly alien to man and to life itself; the more the state is involved in the lives of its citizens, the higher the chance of alienation. Although most socialist thinkers saw the state as a necessity to achieve the socialist utopia, the socialist *Pierre-Joseph Proudhon* was an exception. He thought that property was theft, described himself as an anarchist, and realized that democracy was also not compatible with freedom. He proclaimed that if monarchy is the hammer that crushes the population, then democracy is the axe that divides it. He concluded that both equate to the death of freedom[6]. At least he was consistent with his opinions on the state.

Another guiding principle of socialism is the lack of economic and personal freedom. The abolition of private property is exactly what early socialist thinkers demanded, such as *Gabriel Bonnot de Mably* or *Étienne-Gabriel Morelly,* who, in his utopian socialist work *Code de la Nature,* explains his vision of a perfect world. Everything from food to education is collectivized and organized by the state. He also stressed the importance of the absence of private property and the punishments that those who dared to bring private property into the utopian world would receive. Those people would be kept on burial grounds their entire lives, in separately built cavern-like structures surrounded by walls. When they died, the caverns would be used as tombs[7]. What might seem overly brutal and unnecessary is a thought pattern deeply engrained in socialism.

Most socialist governments have used labor camps and reeducation camps to punish political dissidents and enemies. Although reeducation camps and labor camps were much more common in the twentieth century, countries today, such as communist China and North Korea, evidently still operate reeducation camps and

---

6 *Proudhon* (1848), 85.
7 *Morelly,* (1755/1841), 158, 175.

labor camps. The overarching goal of such camps has always been to create a new human through work and cruel punishment. Due to the lack of natural authority, most socialist states historically had to use violence and fear to establish their authority and scare the population into submission.

Under socialist governments, minorities are hated since they embody the individual. Minorities do not have to be defined exclusively racially. Political, socioeconomic, or religious minorities can embody the status of the enemy just as well. Not spite, but hatred, is the emotion that fuels the socialist. The socialist theme of abolishing established structures and institutions and replacing them with inferior socialist versions is found in the ideology of socialists, such as *Barthélemy-Prosper Enfantin* and his Saint-Simonians, who demanded that all inheritances go to the government, which would then disperse it among the collective[8]. With proper care and planning, families can use inheritances to build a sustainable, intergenerational safety net. The socialist idea is to purge the wealth every generation or have the state leech away at the inheritance until it dissipates completely. The goal being to further weaken the established family structure.

The subsequent step towards comprehending the roots of social democratism is the radical form of international socialism called scientific socialism. An ideology that

---

8   *Pilbeam* (2013), 2.

misunderstands everything from human nature to history. At its core, scientific socialism comprises the same international socialist ideology, with the main difference being that its proponents advocate a revolution and subsequent establishment of a utopia, which they refer to as communism, ruled by the proletariat[9]. This is a collective term for the working class and the poor, whom the socialists have historically favored. One aspect that characterizes the extreme versions of socialism is that, despite their obvious preference for the poor, they rarely come from poor families themselves[10]. The proletariat acts as the counterpart to the bourgeoisie, which personifies the oppressor in the scientific socialist ideology. This dictatorship of the working class would then somehow result in utopia, completely free of capital, which the communists assign a religious meaning to. *Karl Marx,* a hegelian philosopher from a wealthy Jewish family, and his friend *Friedrich Engels,* an investor and son of a wealthy factory owner, are unquestionably the most well-known advocates of communism and scientific socialism.

To contrast his own version of socialism, *Marx* denounced every other form of socialism as unscientific or utopian. This led to the emerging worker associations and especially early social democratic groups being severely weakened during the life of *Marx,* who

---

9   *Winkler* (2000), 143.
10   *Kuehnelt-Leddihn* (1972), 658.

personally attacked and insulted other socialists and denounced their socialist concepts. Communism is what catapulted the socialist worldview from an intellectual movement of disgruntled authors into a religious movement. Communism takes much inspiration from the teachings of *Georg Wilhelm Friedrich Hegel. Marx* interpreted *Hegel's* teachings as a matter of dialectics. This philosopher thought that history was led by dialectical conflicts and contradictions, which would repeal and replace a certain system or idea, which then allegedly fuels history[11].

According to Hegel, who also believed in historicism, not to be confused with historism, history would continue to unfold in a dialectical and circular fashion until one was left with the *absolute,* or what *Marx* refers to as communism. The word revolution comes from the Latin *revolvere* and describes the process of rolling back. This utopian view of unfolding history assumes that people come together under the guise of a theoretical construction of history to change history in their favor[12]. As becomes clear when evaluating the historicist worldview, the opposing dialectical forces must clash together in a revolution to repeal and replace the current system. Even though historicism is a thoroughly flawed ideology, that did not stop Karl Marx from creating his own form of historicism called historical materialism. Like *Hegel, Marx* also included the concept

---

11 Mueller (1958), 413.
12 *Popper* (1957/1986), 47.

of dialectical opposites in his view of history. Unlike *Hegel's* Weltgeist, a form of collective consciousness, *Marx* believed that the social forces would be responsible for literally unfolding history through dialectical materialism. The parallels in their teachings can be explained by *Marx's* fascination with *Hegel's* teachings. Those who read works from both philosophers will know that both consist of more empty phrases and rambling than actual content. *Marx* also believed financial crises emerge because of the falling rate of profit, which then allegedly reduces the amount of lively, value-adding work in the population. This is nothing more than overt nonsense, but the ideology still has believers today.

Karl Marx also took inspiration from *Plato's* innatism, which alleges that humans are already fully formed, with all knowledge readily available to them. Certain experiences could then trigger the human to access his knowledge. Similarly, *Marx* thought that humans could live on a higher plane of existence by establishing communism, which he thought of as the true human form[13]. He wanted to change the world, not just interpret it[14]. This way of thinking provided communist leaders with the argument for killing millions in the name of progress. Killing off the old generation meant unfolding history and getting closer to true communism, which inherently means utopia, without any classes, labor,

---

13 *Marx/Engels* (1844/1968), 546.
14 *Marx/Engels* (1888), 72.

capital, society, culture, or similar concepts of the past. This was the reason why *Marx* thanked the bourgeoisie for weakening the nobility and aristocracy, thereby unfolding history. In the same motion, he also condemns them for allegedly creating the proletariat, thereby sentencing them to their predetermined socialist role as destitute revolutionists. Because communism is also a utopia, every past iteration of socialism is seen as reactionary—in other words, it cannot be real socialism until it is.

Marcuse, part of the Frankfurt School of Critical Theory, which is partially inspired by Marxist doctrine, understands that an increased standard of living leads to the workers having no interest anymore in revolutions since those would also endanger their status-quo[15]. He knew that the old socialism could not radicalize the broad working population anymore. As such, he proposed a new form of socialism in which all marginalized people liberate themselves from their alleged oppressors. Marcuse believes that this can generate enough revolutionary force to lead to the revolution he so desires. Ultimately, critical theory is about liberating oneself from liberty. However, those who try to liberate themselves from liberalism will only end up with socialism.

---

15   *Marcuse/Kellner (ed.)* (2001), 50.

Over time, the socialists became more daring in their actions. When Comparing taxation policies or ideas for taxation under openly socialist people in the late nineteenth century and those from a generation later, such as *Matthias Erzberger* and *Adolf Hitler,* one notices an extreme rise in tax rates. Both for individuals and for corporations. Modern communists understood that groups of people are resilient, even if they strip them of all their belongings. They knew that expropriating people economically is not enough—they must be expropriated culturally as well, to the point that their morals and culture erode over time. Openly communist governments usually reigned in parts of the world where social democratism had not been a powerful or even acknowledged alternative to extreme forms of socialism. An alternative explanation by the communist *Antonio Gramsci* was that communism could only succeed in countries without deeply rooted cultural history, values, and morality. As such, he thought that the new goal of communism should be the subversion of established structures, including through means of subdued change or the elimination of the values and morals that bond the population together. He can be seen as the forefather of the ongoing resurgence of communism, starting in the second half of the twentieth century.

Communists explicitly denounce aid to workers. They

instead advocate letting the conditions deteriorate further. In their eyes, this would lead to the inevitable proletarian revolution faster than if the conditions of the workers improved naturally over time. As this indeed did happen towards the end of *Marx's* life, he did not acknowledge the positive changes that had occurred throughout Europe due to technology and rising productivity. Like *Proudhon*, he was suspicious of a singular governing entity and preferred a government of the proletarian people. Karl Marx was not only against the bourgeoisie but also against Jews. He defined Jews by racial means, believed that the Jewish faith was fueled by money, and worshiped it as their god[16]; they thus had to perish for his communist utopia.

Even though communism is still attached to nature, a certain level of disrespect towards the countryside and those living in it has always been present. In his ten-point measures towards ensuring communism in the communist manifesto, *Marx* advocates the complete urbanization and total alignment of the countryside into the cities[17]. The people of the countryside were fairly autonomous and could not be counted towards the new proletarian class of city inhabitants that *Marx* believed to be the future revolutionaries. Of the other measures he proposed for developed countries, many overlap with the current social democratic reality, such as establishing central banks, central schooling, centralized

---

16   *Marx/Engels* (1981), 374f.
17   *Engels/Marx* (1848), 16.

transportation systems, and a progressive income tax. *Marx's* scientific socialism was against all forms of ‹utopian› socialism, or what he sometimes called bourgeois socialism. Helping the workers without the need for a revolution, similar to the ideas of social democracy, was unacceptable for *Marx* since the proletariat needed to be impoverished before the alleged inevitable revolution. Helping the workers would preserve the bourgeoisie and prevent the revolution of the proletariat. Contemporaries allege that he worked together with the police to get other socialists into trouble[18]. He might have been paid to discredit moderate forms of socialism and prevent progress in the area of social democracy by denouncing all other forms of socialism and alienating potential interested people with his toxicity towards other socialists.

This allegation might be true, especially since *Marx* never got into serious trouble because of his publications, while others were imprisoned. Even though communism was a fringe movement in the nineteenth century, it was vocal enough to prevent serious progress in social democratic movements in the mid-nineteenth century. The alternative was always communist pauperism, which would then scientifically cause all international members of the proletariat to band together and completely overthrow the systems of

---

18   *Vogt* (1859), 166–171.

market and aristocracy in what can only be described as a megalomaniac revolution. Only after *Marx's* death did the social democratic movement grow to considerable size and start slowly overpowering governments in Europe. Even today, governments and other non-governmental organizations fund explicitly radical organizations and movements because the more overpowering something radical becomes, the less likely it is for less radical demands to become fashionable, especially when no compromise is allowed. As such, radical ideas rarely manifest into anything worthwhile when another, more moderate solution exists.

Just like all socialist philosophers and writers before him, *Marx* also tried to discredit private property. He commits the same fallacy that *Rousseau* committed a century earlier. He believes that private property can only exist because some people in the past oppressed others. *Rousseau* was also the one to propagate the theory of the social contract, which is still the basis of legitimacy that social democratic governments use today. The social contract is a concept in which the individual forgoes his rights and property to the collectively governed state.

The general will of the people then decides what is best for the collective. If one can decipher Marx's works, which must have been impossible for the poorly educated workers back then because of the vocabulary and convoluted sentences used in them, one will see how complicated, unnecessary language, constant repetitions, and empty definitions hide the fact that communism does not have much content to begin with. Similarly, in *Karl Marx* Kapital, it is suspected that the poor argumentation can partially be explained by *Marx* retroactively and selectively changing parts of his argumentation to fit the result[19].

This is a practice frowned upon in science, but it might have been the only way for him to create a foundation to base his later argumentation on. The hatred of others more successful than him is exactly what is reflected in *Marx's* image of the bourgeoisie and his socialist ideology of self-hatred. *Marx*, who came from a wealthy family and married the aristocrat *Jenny von Westfalen*, celebrated that the bourgeoisie had caused the downfall of the aristocracy. *Marx*, who came from a Jewish family himself, lived a bourgeoisie rentier lifestyle as a socialist philosopher, had an industrialist as his best friend and partner in crime, and speculated on the stock exchanges[20], while openly despising all those things. He despised everything he embodied. By modern international socialists, he is often seen as a misunderstood revolutionary. Modern national socialists see *Adolf Hitler* in a similar light.

---

19   *von Böhm-Bawerk* (1896/2016), 75f.
20   *Paul/Taylor/Knight/Marsh* (2022), 41.

Recap

- The collective is the most important part of socialism.
- All extreme forms of socialism are inherently racist and anti-Semitic.
- Socialism favors artificial evolution to achieve egalitarianism.
- Not all socialism is extreme. The most important moderate form is social democratism.
- Socialist intellectual forerunners were not poor and disadvantaged.
- Radical socialism is not possible in advanced countries with a wealthy mean population. It is substituted with more moderate forms of socialism.
- Apart from social democratism, the most popular form of international socialism is scientific socialism.
- The scientifically socialist end goal is the utopian condition of communism.
- Progress in radical forms of international socialism can only occur through revolution because the ideology subscribes to historicism.

3. NATIONAL SOCIALISM

Because socialists have always attributed the negative values of so-called capitalism to the Jews, they inherently have an anti-Semitic and racist history[21]. Intellectual leaders of socialism have all advocated genocide to some degree, whether that is a religious, cultural, racial, or economic kind. Their followers, maybe unknowingly, continue to enable these destructive ideologies, often forgetting that egalitarianism can only succeed when different people are artificially denied their natural rights to life, liberty, and property. Denying the politically left heritage of international socialist racism and genocide is an intense form of cognitive dissonance and selective attention to facts, present in many international socialists today. Especially those who try to shift the entire blame on their national equivalent. Most modern national socialists suffer from a similar fallacy. They try to discard the evidence of national socialist crimes by accusing everyone of forging documents and alleging that the national socialists simply fought the assumed world conspiracy, usually consisting of everyone but the national socialists themselves. Radical national socialist

---

21   *Green* (1985), 381f.

dictators, such as *Mussolini* or *Hitler,* did not like the thought of international socialism and decided it was in the best interest of their subordinates for the government to pursue the politics of national socialism. They achieve this by combining socialism with nationalism, the perverted, politically left form of patriotism. Although unsucessful in the early years, national socialism soon became an alternative to communism and social democratism—both of which already had a large following in the early 1920s Weimar Republic.

In current times, many people have serious trouble differentiating between the political right and left. Everything slightly deviating from the social democratic norm is deemed radical, right-wing, populist, or everything at once. If one believes in the outdated and unhelpful two-dimensional political spectrum, most ruling political ideologies today are politically left, while true right-wing ideologies comprise a marginal percentage of any given population: people who are anti-democratic, value liberty over the state, and who also favor a strong constitution. Some people go so far as to say that national socialists such as *Mussolini, Hitler,* and associates were politically right. This is on par with historical revisionism and could not be further from the truth. The national socialist ideology, similar to international socialism, seeks to liberate the people. In this case, they were to be liberated from the oppressive forces of the Treaty of Versailles and from Judaism, which was allegedly oppressing the German people.

Joseph Goebbels, an important national socialist, spoke out against the free market, liberalism, the Jews, and Marxism. International socialism, such as communism or social democratism, he saw as a ruse of Jewish thought, which would allegedly divert attention from socialism to class warfare. He opposed the free market as it prevented full employment, especially during the 1920s and 1930s when the unemployment rate reached 30 percent. He believed that only the combination of socialism and nationalism would allow for a truly free population, free of wage slavery[22]. Furthermore, he thought of liberalism as a dying ideology to be replaced by socialism. His influential role as minister of propaganda and public education under the regime of the *NSDAP* meant that his opinions were funneled through radio, newspapers, and mainstream thought at the time. His combination of intense and irrational hatred of certain groups and the ability to perpetuate self-victimization in the population made him a perfect propaganda minister.

Calling socialism right-wing is one example of low-level disinformation that many have fallen for today. The argumentation is riddled with logical mistakes and, as such, is debunked easily. First, it is established that right-wing people are anti-socialist. Then it is noticed that national socialists have prosecuted other competing

---

22   *Goebbels* (1932), 15.

socialists. It is then inferred, that the national socialists must be right-wing. Another debunked claim propagated by socialist historians was that industrialists of the early twentieth century orchestrated the downfall of the Weimar Republic to assist *Hitler* in his rise to power and were fundamental in funding his party during that time. Having a proper understanding of the political sphere at the time is important to understand why this is false. It can be assumed that those who still propagate these false theories today are either guided by mischievous motivations or simply do not have the necessary historical knowledge. To deliberately disinform people about the origins of socialism, most modern socialists try to disassociate national socialism with their own ideology by calling it nazism, which conceals the socialist identity of the ideology, or denouncing any ties to socialism entirely by suggesting it is not real socialism.

There is a certain truth in the mistrust between the Weimar Republic and owners of large businesses in the 1920s. These owners were not fond of the Weimar Republic, which embodied the newly achieved social democracy. That being said, the people responsible for helping the *National Socialist German Workers' Party (NSDAP)* gain more power and those who weakened the republic were politicians who were responsible for the disastrous situation in the 1920s. Additionally, politicians of the *Kampffront Schwarz-Weiß-Rot (KSWR)*, consisting of the *Deutschnationale Volkspartei (DNVP)*,

Stahlhelm, and *Landbund,* entered into a coalition with the *NSDAP* in 1933. The *KSWR* was becoming increasingly irrelevant compared to the extreme parties in the political landscape. Because the Weimar Republic went from crisis to crisis, it did not last long compared to previous iterations of Germany. The unfortunate combination of hyperinflation, war reparations, and high unemployment provided an unstable political sphere and breeding grounds for the radical left-wing parties to prosper. By the time the *NSDAP* and the *KSWR* formed a parliament in 1933, all liberal parties were gone or had been completely marginalized by being assimilated into bigger parties. The middle-class business owners of the 1920s and 1930s mostly opposed large businesses, as these had the means to establish cartels more easily and prevent smaller competition from operating on the market at non-cartel prices. The national socialists promised these small business owners more influence in the economic endeavors at the time.

As such, some small business owners felt inclined to vote for the *NSDAP.* However, because the 1920s and 1930s were challenging times and presented the population with hyperinflation, economic corrections, and high unemployment, few of these small business owners had large amounts of money with which they could have funded the party in any substantial manner. Because of the harsh economic corrections, most party members paid only their membership fees. Additional donations were rare at the time, especially in the early years of the NSDAP. In later years, the membership fees were increased after the party realized it could charge its members much higher fees. The owners of large businesses were mostly liberal and had their own interests in mind. As such, accusing them of funding a small but openly socialist party to rise to power is overt nonsense. It is clear that most owners of large businesses back then acknowledged the party as politically left and compartmentalized the political views of the national socialists with those of social democrats and communists[23]. Other terms that were used to describe the national socialists were conspiratorial, demagogic, and terroristic[24]. It is obvious that the business owners did not fall for *Hitler's* empty demagogic phrases, and any attempt to mark him as an agent for ‹the capital›, is evidently a sad attempt to distort history in favor of international socialism.

Only after the 1930 election and the associated rise of the *NSDAP* did owners of large businesses start to perceive the party as a serious threat. Some of them started donating small amounts of money to the party, which was not uncommon in the political sphere of the Weimar Republic. They believed that they could curb the radical development in the party by donating to specific national socialists, whom they thought of as moderate enough to influence the party in their interests—but to no avail. Although all documents that discuss the

---

23   *Zitelmann* (2017), 325.
24   *Turner* (1985), 114.

NSDAP's finances in depth were destroyed shortly before WW2 ended, by using the few documents and secret police reports still available, one has the ability to recreate parts of the *NSDAP's* financial situation. Even though the *NSDAP* had existed since 1919, only after 1928 did the party become substantially relevant in German politics at the time. As such, it is disappointing to see no comprehensive data for these years. According to two police reports regarding the general meeting of the party, the internal revenue between February 1925 and April 30th, 1926, totaled 55,000 Mark, while the internal expenditures totaled 54,700 Mark[25]. At the end of the fiscal year 1927, the party totaled 254,996 Mark of revenue, while the expenditures totaled 252,146 Mark[26].

The financial situation of the *NSDAP* was quite pitiful in the first few years. Although the *NSDAP* seemed to have about 100,000 members by early 1928, the party's massive growth did not set in until 1930. The *NSDAP* increased their membership fees dramatically that same year. While previously the monthly membership fee was 80 Reichspfennig, starting in 1930, the minimum membership fee increased to 1.20 Reichsmark, and the party gave their members the option to give up to five Reichsmark or even more if they so desired. The national socialists also had great success with their assemblies, in which they demanded a one Reichsmark

25   NSDAP (1926/2013).
26   NSDAP (1926/2013).

fee to enter[27]. Much evidence points towards the *NSDAP* having fewer members in its early years than the *Social Democratic Party of Germany (SPD)*, but being on par with them by 1930.

The NSDAP realized they could easily demand more money from their members. Their revenue seems to have increased massively after the 1930 elections, due to their party skyrocketing in popularity. This gave them higher revenue than the *SPD* had at the time[28]. After Hitler became chancellor of the Weimar Republic, *Hermann Göring* orchestrated a meeting with industry representatives, supposedly to have *Hitler* explain his politics to them in private. In reality, the meeting was a ruse to beg for donations from the attendees. *Hjalmar Schacht,* a prominent banker and politician who later joined the NSDAP and was both minister of economy and president of the Reichsbank, presented a bill of exchange amounting to three million Reichsmark. The money was to be split between the NSDAP and the KSWR.

In the end, only two million Reichsmark were actually collected[29] and then split between the two parties. In addition to the one-time donation, after the NSDAP had already taken over the Weimar Republic, an initiative of a German industry association was set up that proposed

---

27   *Zitelmann* (2022), 214.
28   *Matzerath/Turner* (1977), 64, 70.
29   *Nuernberg military tribunals* (1953), 556, 567f.

a voluntary donation to *Adolf Hitler* from their members. For the year 1933, the members were expected to donate 0.5 percent of the total annual wages paid to their employees in the previous year[30]. Although the donation was meant to be exclusive to the year 1933, it later became an annual forced payment. At that point, the national socialists already had authority over the tax revenue, and their own industries supplied them with additional income, so this forced donation merely supplemented it.

Not large businesses, but politicians and policymakers, were responsible for the dire situation that brought the *NSDAP* to power[31]. Especially *Heinrich Brüning, Franz von Papen,* and *Kurt von Schleicher* played a fundamental role in establishing *Adolf Hitler* as the chancelor of the Weimar Republic and therefore allowing the *NSDAP* to take absolute control. Mostly communists, socialists, and people tied to post-World War II socialist regimes tried to prove that the *NSDAP* had been funded and brought to power by wealthy industrialists. Even going so far as to falsify *Hitler's* quotes by combining different parts of speeches and sentences, or by fabricating them entirely[32]. Whoever still believes in these debunked hoaxes is being dishonest enough to knowingly publish disinformation or simply cannot be bothered to study the available material.

---

30 *ZBW Press Archives* (n.d.).
31 *Turner* (1985), 341.
32 *Walden* (1960), 25.

On an economic level, the national socialists, after coming to power, were interested in full employment—as are social democrats today. To get to full employment, the national socialists granted companies tax credits whenever they employed new people. To be able to employ more people, the government granted these companies the ability to employ workers at lower wages than previously established by tariffs[33]. Although many have fallen for the propaganda that suggests the economy was prosperous during the party's reign, in reality, real wages during the *NSDAP's* reign were lower than in previous years[34]. The high-employment schemes worked temporarily by employing people in the state sector. But they did not create long-term, sustainable workplaces for the population. The *NSDAP* taxed some businesses directly, while taxing other owners of partnerships directly with their personal income tax rate.

The taxes for businesses steadily rose from the old Weimar Republic rate of 20 percent to 55 percent by 1942. Compared to the tax rates for businesses, the progressive personal income tax was increased to 65 percent[35]. Because of special war taxes, including a 50 percent tax on the existing income tax[36], *Banken* (2018) establishes in his research that the effective tax rate for

---

33   *Sahm* (2018), 293.
34   *Bry* (1960), 467.
35   *Banken* (2018), 404–408.
36   Kriegswirtschaftsverordnung vom 4. September 1939
      (RGBl. I S.1609).

some business owners came close to 90 percent, not including mandatory donations and other taxes[37]— hardly conditions one could describe as a free economy. The central government used the majority of the tax revenue, while the provinces, states, and communities were given only a fraction of the total revenue.

Although tax revenue increased tremendously every single year except from 1943–44 onwards, Banken (2018) concludes that tax revenue alone was not sufficient to finance their operations and fight the war. The national socialist government progressively used more debt as the years went by[38], to finance their operations and compensate for the high spending, which led to another bout of inflation during the war. The Jewish part of the population had to pay higher tax rates than non-Jews. In later years, Jewish property and companies were directly expropriated and liquidated to generate revenue for the government.

Additionally, homeowners had to collectively pay billions of Reichsmark[39] to persuade the government to stop levying a tax on homeowners who ‹benefited› from the hyperinflation. The tax, *Gebäudeentschuldungssteuer*, was levied to punish those who had their debt erased because of the hyperinflation. When the aforementioned

---

37   Banken (2018), 413f.
38   Banken (2018), 32–36, 357.
39   Verordnung über die Aufhebung der Gebäudeentschuldungsst euer vom 31. Juli 1942 (RGBl I S. 501).

regulation was passed to stop the tax from being levied, the homeowners had to collectively pay the yearly revenue tenfold in exchange. In general, there was a definite difference in the extent to which the German part and the non-German part of the population were subjected to taxation.

With each passing year, the severity of taxation increased for the minorities. Other legislation was passed to oppress the Jewish part of the German population. The *Nürnberger Rassengesetze*[40] were largely based on old Catholic Canon Law, which penalized Jewish people just as much, if not more. After the legislation was passed, Jews no longer had the right to bear positions in the civil service, they could not vote, they were not allowed to marry non-Jews and they had no permission to hoist the new German flag. Over the years, the legislation was changed and reinforced multiple times, but the Jewish population had fewer civil rights with each iteration of the legislation.

Even though the national socialists were not fond of universal welfare, they did introduce legislation that provided welfare to the German part of the population, including cheap health insurance, child benefits, and the other already established forms of welfare from the

---

40   Reichsflaggengesetz vom 15. September 1935
      (RGBl. I S. 1145); Reichsbürgergesetz vom 15. September
      1935 (RGBl. I S. 1146); Gesetz zum Schutze des deutschen
      Blutes und der deutschen Ehre vom 15. September 1935
      (RGBl. I S. 1146).

previous regimes. Because the NSDAP placed the common good of the nation before the personal good, they naturally expanded the welfare legislation for Germans while strengthening their socialist ‹Volkskörper›. Because individual initiative is subordinated to the collective under socialist governments, the national socialist government dissolved and banned all private unions and replaced them with their own national socialist equivalent, which did not act as a real union for workers but rather was a collective of employees and employers who were directly subordinated to the government. It had the authority to change employment contracts, set wages, and regulate who worked where. After 1934, people were not allowed to choose their own workplace anymore, and 1938 saw the increase of compulsory working hours[41].

Everything workplace-related was regulated, and private property had been completely hollowed out. Business owners *de jure* were degraded to managers instead of retaining absolute authority over their property. The socialists in the Weimar Republic were quite militant in general and were all willing to fight each other[42] [43]. The national socialists, the communists, and the social democrats all fought with each other in street fights to secure potential voters for their own

---

41   *Schmidt/Ostheim/Siegel/Zohlnhöfer (Eds.)* (2007), 145.
42   BT WD 1 - 3010 – 017/17, 49.
43   *Vossische Zeitung* (04.05.1929), 1.

parties and demoralize the other parties. In those fights and disputes, it was not uncommon for people to become severely injured or even die.

Another claim is that the national socialists advocated the free market and allegedly reprivatized banks that were nationalized before. Nationalizations are a form of expropriation that usually follows through forcefully, without much, if any, compensation. The claim that they carried out privatizations is unfounded and another attempt at distorting history. Because of the inflationary post-World War I environment, the German banks found themselves in deep trouble. The term bailout has a deep contemporary connection with the banking sector, especially since fractional-reserve banking has seen much greater and more excessive use in recent decades compared to previous centuries.

Because the *Darmstädter und Nationalbank*—one of the biggest German banks in the 1920s and early 1930s—had to file insolvency in 1931, the government of the Weimar Republic was inclined to bail out the *Dresdner Bank* in order to prevent the complete downfall of the banking sector. In the case of the *Dresdner Bank*, one of the largest banks in Germany during the 1930s, the government thought that stabilizing the bank would help curb the massive bank runs that were taking place at the time. As such, they decided not to nationalize the bank, as this would have constituted a loss of trust among the population. Instead, the government bailed out the bank with 300 million Reichsmark in the form of holding preferred stock in the company with seven percent dividends and preference in dividends. The government paid the money in treasury bills with maturities of one to three years and rates of seven percent[44]. Contrary to popular belief, the German government did not sell its shares in the bank to generate revenue. Instead, the bank bought back their shares in the company from the government because it was more financially sound than in previous years and had recovered from the economic corrections of the early 1930s.

This is typical after bailouts, as the companies are interested in controlling the company themselves and will buy back shares or pay back the money until they can assume full control again. Similar to the *Dresdner Bank*, albeit not as serious, the *Deutsche Bank und Disconto-Gesellschaft* and the *Commerz- und Privat-Bank* were also bailed out by the government. The two banks later bought back their shares as well. Other notable examples of supposed reprivatization, full or partial, under national socialist leadership are the *Vereinigte Stahlwerke/Gelsenkirchener Bergwerks-AG* and the *Deutsche Reichsbahn*. The *Deutsche Reichsbahn* was constructed as a joint-stock company from the beginning in 1924[45], because the government wanted

---

44   *Bähr* (2006), 50.
45   Gesetz über die Deutsche Reichsbahn-Gesellschaft
      (Reichsbahngesetz) vom 30. August 1924 (RGBl. II S. 272).

the company to be profitable. Of the 15 billion Reichsmark capital stock, two were preferred stock and thirteen were common stock owned directly by the state. The alleged privatization was simply people buying preferred stock in the company. The public company was never privatized. Even if all the preferred shares were sold, the state would still own the absolute majority of the company. After a hasty bailout of the *Vereinigte Stahlwerke* in 1932, similar to the *Dresdner Bank* or *Commerz- und Privatbank,* the company wanted to repurchase their shares in 1936. In those years, joint-stock companies were only allowed to repurchase their stocks to the extent of 10 percent of their capital stock[46]. Because the shares amounted to more than 10 percent, legislation was passed to allow the large transaction to pass[47].

Conflating nationalizations with bailouts does occur frequently, especially when avid readers and even historians do not have access to the primary sources and have to rely on translations. In the case of the national socialists, it is fair to assume malice when others accuse them of nationalization. This is another way that international socialists try to distance themselves from their national equivalent—without success. *Hitler* despised liberalism and the free market. He thought of

---

46   Verordnung des Reichspräsidenten über Aktienrecht, Bankenaufsicht und über eine Steueramnestie vom 19. September 1931 (RGBl. I S. 493, 663).
47   Gesetz über den Erwerb eigener Aktien vom 14. Mai 1936 (RGBl. I S. 439).

the liberal bourgeoisie as weak and subservient[48]—perhaps up until members of the political right tried to assassinate him in 1944. He admitted afterwards that he failed to assume control of the political right, whom he previously did not see as a threat, due to his perception of them as weak and cowardly. Just like *Marx*, he associated the free market with the interests of Jewish international capital and thus was not inclined to allow economic freedom or the freedom of the Jewish faith. Although the *NSDAP* did allow people whose property served the common good to keep it, that right was tied to their standing in the Volksgemeinschaft, which excluded Jews, political dissidents, minorities, and other people that the *NSDAP* deemed non-Arian or asocial. The *NSDAP* regularly made use of its authority to seize property and command businesses.

Whenever companies were not willing or able to accomplish the government's goals, they were seized by the government or controlled by members of the party. Most business owners would have rather cooperated than have their companies seized. In addition to the massive industrial complex under the immediate authority of the national socialists, the party had its own government-run companies, such as the *Reichswerke Hermann Göring,* one of the biggest companies in the world at the time. The *NSDAP* also did not shy away from allocating slave labor to various companies, both

---

48   *Hitler* (1925/1927), 590.

their own and those under private management. They even made use of their government authority by expropriating Jewish businesses and selling them to other Germans while purposefully valuing the businesses at a fraction of their market value. Later, they were liquidated directly, showing how little regard they had for property rights and the free market. The party saw property, businesses, and people as mere means to complete their goals, using forced cooperation and association in the form of the *Deutsche Arbeitsfront.* Their absolute governmental authority over all the property and businesses, including the expropriative taxation measures, price controls, and corporate surveillance, certainly did not allow for even remotely market-like conditions.

Adolf Hitler started as a dedicated socialist who, with increasing exposure to the political aparatus, realized that he wanted to create a new political extreme *sui generis* to succeed with his plan to assume power. He believed that only by establishing a new national socialist standard could he overcome the alleged limitations of international socialism, set new priorities, and disregard all the established reactionary structures and institutions of liberalism and the aristocracy. National socialism is a socialist ideology that tries to strike a balance between full state control and useful liberal institutions that can benefit the state, although the latter were hollowed out with increased exposure to the national socialist legislative and political apparatus.

RECAP

- The national socialists were not brought to power by industrialists.
- The unstable environment of the Weimar Republic is to blame for the rise of the NSDAP.
- National socialism is the national equivalent of international socialism.
- The NSDAP massively increased tax rates for individuals and companies.
- Under the rule of the national socialists, property was completely hollowed out.
- At no point can the national socialist economy be described as a market economy. It was a picture-perfect planned economy.
- The national socialists did not reprivatize companies.
- Minorities were explicitly prevented from assuming certain positions, their property was confiscated and sold, and their taxes were higher than usual.
- In socialist fashion, the NSDAP mass-killed minorities, as seen under other extreme socialist governments.

4. SOCIAL DEMOCRATISM

After World War II, a milder form of socialism, called social democratism, became increasingly popular around the world and was adopted by most Western governments. Because few people acknowledge the movement's history, many are perplexed by the fact that social democratic governments are showing a concerning trend towards socialism. Contrary to popular belief, social democracy is not the third way between socialism and the free market. Social democrats are fueled by a kind of progressivism.

The kind that is alleged to occur naturally but must be nudged in the correct direction anyway, in tiny incremental steps[49]. Social democrats nowadays tend to feel the need to democratize[50] other nations with different values. What were once the crusades is now the war on drugs, poverty, crime, etc., with the end goal being to democratize the enemy—peacefully. The argument that democracies are peaceful is perhaps one of the more delirious attempts at arguing in favor of such a system. Those people simply must look at the last 100 years of wars, deaths, poverty, and economic

---

49   *von Kuehnelt-Leddihn* (1985/2019), 324f.
50   *Somary* (1984/2010), 147f.

planning, in the name of the people and democracy, to fully dismiss the notion of democracies being inherently more peaceful than their non-socialist counterparts.

Many contemporary issues are rooted in social democratism. The undifferentiated discourse on this topic is dangerous for the plurality of opinions. Yet social democracy is usually left unquestioned or seen as an adequate compromise. Even fewer people know what implications social democracy is based on. Leaving such ideologies unquestioned without resolving their history creates massive opportunities for states and institutions to exploit large parts of the gullible population. Criticism of the system itself is scarce, especially in public discourse. Governments across the globe have put enormous resources into forming and influencing the political opinions of the population, as explained in chapter one.

The resulting relationship between citizen and democracy creates a toxic and highly politicized environment, absent of liberalism, that populism thrives in. Social democratism severely fragments and radicalizes the population in the process. Defining social democracy seems simple enough at first. It becomes harder the second one tries to define *social* as a specific term. It has no standalone meaning since it constantly changes depending on the time and person asked[51], and it has to be used as a prefix in conjunction with another

---

51   *von Hayek/Bartley III (ed.) (1988)*, 114.

word to retain any meaning at all. As presently defined by one of the first social democratic parties, social democracy and democratic socialism can and should be used interchangeably[52][53][54]. That creates a strong correlation between the terms social and socialism, which needs to be investigated further.

Democratism and its manifestation as democracy, the underlying ideology, is usually translated to ‹the power of the people›, allegedly stemming from the old Greek word *δημοκρᾰτία*, supposedly being split into the words *δῆμος* and *κράτος*. This idea is ridiculous and grammatically incorrect. The original meaning of *δῆμος* is ‹to divide›. The Attican politician *Κλεισθένης* thought that power must be fragmented so that no one person can usurp all the power. He divided ancient Attica into ‹demes›, which were district-like plots of land. The term *κράτος* means ‹to have strength or might›. When combining the two terms with the suffix -*ία* to form a feminine noun, one is left with a noun that describes a political system that divides power.

This system of *δημοκρᾰτία* did not have the power of the people in mind. Abductive reasoning is to blame for the behavior of people who use their current understanding of democracy and project it onto Ancient Attica. In the ancient system, multiple of the demes formed a *τριττύς*,

---

52   *SPD* (2007), 16f.
53   *SPD* (1989/1998), 52.
54   *SPD* (1959), 8.

or a third. These thirds, from the city, the countryside, and the coast, amounted to a φυλή, or tribe. In total, ten tribes existed, each of which sent fifty representatives, who were supposed to represent the tribes in the βουλευταί, a form of parliament. In total, these 500 people were all selected by lot. The randomness was supposed to aid in fragmenting the power. Direct and equal voting of representatives, as is commonplace in modern social democracies, was never the goal in that system. The ἐκκλησία, a small assembly of a fraction of the Attican population, met a few times a month to discuss important issues. It had the ability to hold the magistrates accountable after their one-year term. In reality, the modern democracy has its beginnings in the old Germanic tradition of the *ting*, which was a regular meeting or assembly that discussed important issues and acted as a court that resolved conflicts between persons[55].

The modern understanding of democracy is not to divide power by randomly choosing representatives. Instead, the power must be concentrated in elected representatives, completely voted for by choice. Lobbying is prevalent, populism wins over rational ideas and logic, and short-term thinking is key in modern democracies. It is the ideal self-congratulatory system for the conceited masses—at least when their favorite party wins. The *Socialdemocratic Workers' Party (SDAP)*

---

55   *von Mayenburg (ed.)* (2021), 454.

thought that only the democratic state could solve the problems of the nineteenth century[56]—thus avoiding revolutionary tendencies and the bloodshed that other forms of socialism inevitably lead to. The idea was quite noble, compared to other extreme socialist ideologies. People living under social democratic governments live relatively free, albeit restricted. Although freedom indices that try to calculate scores exist, they are mostly flawed. The indices try to quantify qualitative data, such as emotions or quality of legislation, and they all fail to reflect the difference between reality *de jure* and *de facto* in the presented countries.

The indices also do not evaluate implicit debt, unreported corruption, real wages, the effect of regulation, state liability, or manipulated unemployment statistics. That being said, compared to absolute monarchies with god-given rulers and socialist regimes with party-given rulers, people living under social democracy can, at least, vote for their own paternalists within the social democratic regulatory framework. This is fine if every person is a social democrat at heart. Although the social democratic movement became much more popular around the world after World War II, it was certainly not new at the time, having been founded as an openly socialist movement in the nineteenth century with strong ties to communism[57].

---

56   *SDAP* (1947), 121.
57   *Bookchin* (1998), 278f.

The idea of social democratism, or democratic socialism, was to improve the lives and working conditions of workers using policies, without explicitly expropriating the property of all owners. In the early years, the movement focused on providing self-help organizations on a local level. This quickly shifted by the late 1860s, and the international focus within the movement became apparent. The *General German Workers' Association* even demanded a solidaric European state. This differs substantially from the current European Union but is not far off from the idea of establishing a united European state under the guise of the United States of Europe, which would reduce the national member state to a vassal state without the right to secede from the Union. That being said, the Treaty of Lisbon has once again increased the parallels of the EU primary law to those of a constitution, although it is still a *sui generis* organization and not a state.

The early programs of the *Socialdemocratic Workers' Party* denounced national boundaries and saw social democratism as a social task, encompassing all countries that had modern life. Like most socialists, however, they wanted to terminate the concept of the wage system and demanded that communal work replace it. Starting in their first 1869 program, the party demanded a progressive income tax in combination with having all indirect taxes abolished. They called for an equal right to vote for all men aged twenty and above and equality before the law. Starting in the 1890s, they also demanded equal rights for women. Equality before the law and improving working conditions were certainly the *Socialdemocratic Party of Germany*'s main goals, regardless of its questionable methods, demands, and name, which had previously been the *Socialist Workers' Party* and *Socialdemocratic Workers' Party*, until 1890. In their 1891 *Erfurter Programm*, they demanded the eight-hour day and started proclaiming that private property was completely incompatible with the social democratic movement and needed to be turned into common property[58], letting their radical socialist ties shine through and shedding their more moderate demands of previous pamphlets. The social democratic demands stayed largely the same in between the 1891 *Erfurter Programm*, the 1921 *Görlitzer Programm*, and the 1925 *Heidelberger Programm*. That being said, they became more specific in regard to their policies. By 1921, the program had evolved from a simple ten- to fifteen-point program to a more elaborate pamphlet.

Ferdinand Lassalle, a Hegelian and one of the founders of the social democratic movement, saw social democracy as a more national movement. He was more nationally oriented than communists such as *Marx* and *Engels* and propagated worker self-help and using the democratic government to achieve goals through policies instead of communist proletarian dictatorship and complete liquidation of all non-proletarians and private property,

---

58   *Marx/Engels* (1919), 32.

as other socialist associates had suggested. He had connections to *Fürst von Bismarck* and proposed ideas for a social democratic monarchy. Something that *Bismarck* started to achieve himself in the 1890s through legislation that established compulsory insurance. In that sense, Lassalle was a moderate national socialist, although he did not define his socialism racially, like the *NSDAP*. While he was alive, there was a strong competition between *Marx* and himself. Because *Lasalle* was Jewish, *Marx* insulted him in private letters to *Engels*, in which he commented on *Lassalle's* supposed negroid and Jewish appearance[59]. *Lassalle* thought that the general right to vote was supposed to aid in establishing the socialist system, which would inevitably lead to social change. The individualism present in liberal doctrine was to be removed by marginalizing individual opinion and subordinating it to the democratic process of collective decision-making. The transition to socialism was to be led by a dictator who helped nudge society in the ‹correct› direction through peaceful reforms.

Liberalism is generally seen as archaic and reactionary in socialist literature, since it embodies the antithesis of collectivism and advocates liberty instead of liberation. Although *Lassale's* idea seems to conflict with modern democratic principles, his argument was logically sound because he believed in *Hegel's* and *Rodbertus'* teachings.

---

59   *Marx/Engels* (1974), 257.

To him, it was mandatory that a strong dictator save the working population through state socialism and social reforms. He did not believe that masses of people could establish socialism—only the state could. His early death in 1864, however, prevented him from further shaping the socialist doctrine or from having any lasting influence in the nineteenth century. His doctrine became widely known only after *Marx* died, who suppressed many other socialist theorists during his lifetime. During *Karl Marx*'s life, the social democratic movement was undermined and attacked constantly by him, even though scientific socialism only had little influence on the actual working population.

World War I seemingly warranted inflating the money supply on a large scale, in addition to voiding the gold standard still present in many countries at the time. After World War II, most social democracies had already implemented numerous socialist policies, from centralized schooling to progressive taxation. To appease the European royalty, it was allowed to play a non-political representative role in some social democracies, although their wealth and property were often confiscated or expropriated to ensure a considerable loss of power. Even today, many families have not yet been able to reclaim their property, while a few, at least, were given the chance to repurchase it from the state. With monarchy and aristocracy out of the question, the communists were the only militant and openly violent political demagogues in the post-World

War II political sphere who could harm the social democratic movement. The true liberal political positions died out when the last proper monarchies in Europe ceased to exist, and the social democrats became the driving political force. The vast majority of people still representing the liberal system died within the twentieth century. As such, the longer the system of social democracy continues, the harder it becomes to simulate political opposition, leading to the crazy disinformation of alternative media that is supposed to act as a counterpart to social democratic opinion. After all, it is hard to simulate opposition, with the only acknowledged political opinion being one on the range between moderate social democrat and more extreme social democrat. No matter how many social democratic parties exist, their singular existence will always limit political discourse to a range of allowable opinions. Allowable, in this context, does not mean being the only opinion not punished by legal measures. It describes an intellectually precarious situation in which the mean population is the political guarantor of allowable opinion.

In recent decades, the arch-ideology of communism seems to be experiencing a renaissance through covert communism, thereby defeating the purpose of the struggle in the twentieth century between social democratism and communism. Examples include the Cold War, organizations such as the *World Anti-Communist League*, anti-communist counterintelligence operations, or banning openly communist parties from social democratic parliaments—at least in some states. The struggle between communism and social democratism is old and might have been one reason for the *NSDAP's* successful election results in the early 1930s. The communists, who accused the social democrats of being social fascists[60], fought the social democrats just as much as their other competitor, the national socialists. Post-World War II, the social democratic movement within Europe was becoming bigger. Even though quite a few European countries had social democratic unions and some had established parties in the nineteenth century, the unquestionable beginnings of social democracy were in Germany.

Unsurprisingly, all social democratic parties, current and past, have eerily similar pamphlets and agendas. As such, one can apply the same teachings of social democracy analogously to parties in other countries. The movement only grew to its current size in the twentieth century, which is when many other European countries started to establish their own social democratic parties and the ideology spread to most First-World countries. The *Christian Democratic Union* relativized private property in a social democratic fashion, demanded a social reorganization of property and rights[61] and wanted to overcome capitalism and

---

60   *Draper* (1972), 335.
61   *CDU* (1946), 5.

Marxism[62]. The *SPD* completely reformed their party in later years. They cut ties with parts of the previous, more radical programs discussed above but kept true to their communist roots. They were aware that the social democratic movement was not in a position to become more radical. In hegelian fashion, the social democrats, both the *CDU* and *SPD*, took the free market, combined it with socialism, and were left with the social market economy, a bastardized version of two systems, neither of which could fully operate. This is dialectical materialist thought; they believe that overcoming and resolving these contradictions will lead to human progress[63].

Although supposedly liberal parties such as the *Free Democratic Party* were less inclined to fall for the dialectical doctrine, at first, they soon were ideologically assimilated into the social democratic movement. Similar developments can be perceived in other European social democracies and even in the United States, especially after the New Deal in the 1930s. The *Socialdemocatic Party of Germany*'s openly communist ties were only officially denounced in 1959, after the *Godesberger Programm*, which explicitly distanced the party and ideology from communism[64], since it was becoming unfashionable for social democrats to be connected with communism, which had caused so much

---

62   *CDU* (1947), 3.
63   *Popper* (1994), 253.
64   *SPD* (1959), 8.

destruction even up until that point. The party also explicitly acknowledged that socialism can only be realized through democracy and *vice versa*. Therefore, democratic socialism and social democratism are congruent terms and refer to the same concept. Social democracies could never denounce socialism without denouncing themselves.

This event marked a shift that allowed for the definite primacy of social democracy in First-World countries. Although there had been opposition from the political right before, the democratic system of different political opinions had effectively been abolished. Although there were still different parties available, their differences were marginal, unimportant, and superficial. Social democracies necessitate that everything possible be democratically legitimized. Officially, the term democratic legitimization suggests that political discourse between the many social democratic parties ultimately leads to a satisfactory social democratic solution. The *a priori* argument is that the decision is legitimate simply because some voters have voted for specific political parties or candidates.

This argument is false since voting can only portray opinions, not legitimize them. If one sheep and three wolves vote on who should be eaten as dinner, the democratic result will not be morally just, or particularly convincing, since the majority is able to suppress the minority with the power of a vote. This is assumed to be a representative democracy. That it is quite demeaning to vote for one's own political paternalist, and be told that this is a privilege, is typically not considered. The winning parties and candidates only represent those who voted for them, not the whole population. If the political party X receives twenty-five percent of the votes, eighty percent of eligible voters have voted, and seventy percent of the population is eligible to vote, the original twenty-five percent actually only comprises fourteen percent of the total population. If one adds in whether the politicians keep their campaign promises and the influence of interposing organizations and lobbying, one will end up with sub-one percent rates of democratic legitimization in any given social democracy. Unless everyone is eligible to vote, participation is at one hundred percent, and everyone votes the same, democratically legitimate decisions cannot exist.

In a similar fashion, paying taxes also does not warrant unwavering support for the governing entities, since the nature of taxation establishes that the payment is involuntary and enforced through violence. As such, the main problem with legitimizing legislation is that it can only bind those who sign it. Otherwise, everyone could create legislation and force others to live by it. This also directly critiques *Rousseau's* idea of a social contract, in which the whole population voluntarily transfers some of their freedoms to the state, thinking that this would result in more freedom. Although others try to attribute a fictional monopoly on power to the state, this concept is little more than wishful thinking. When one thinks of countries such as Switzerland and the United States, which comprise large percentages of armed citizens, it becomes clear why a monopoly on power can only be upheld as long as the citizens do not revolt. The question of democratic legitimacy is quite important to social democrats. Without it, they would be no better than normal socialists, who have no moral trouble overthrowing the status quo and shaping it according to their own ideas. The supposed pillars of social democracy are fundamentally broken by design. They have been purposely constructed to warrant little protection—in only the most basic areas of life—from the government while allowing the government to violate the entire population within that legal framework. To ensure that the population is unable to properly and fully prosecute the government, it created its own legislation to guarantee that it is not subjected to the same terrible legislation that it subjects its citizens to.

If one further evaluates the argument of democratic legitimization, then multiple layers of voting cannot be less democratic than one layer, under the assumption that there is a direct democratic link between the voter and the elected. Elected representatives should then be able to vote for their own representatives. This process could then continue indefinitely, or until there exists only one more person who represents everyone else. It is uncertain whether the average person in the population would accept this, though. *Niccolò Machiavelli* and *David Hume* both realized that a simple democratic government cannot function long-term because of its shortcomings. Instead, they advocated a government with additional elements of monarchy and aristocracy. Even the old Roman Republic had all three elements. Another reason why voting is unable to legitimize the government is that arbitrary age minimums for voting fundamentally oppose the democratic principle of universal and free suffrage. The periods of abstinence from voting usually vary anywhere from three to six years and are arbitrary yet again, based only on what seems acceptable to the mean population. Even if people are allowed to vote, they will never be able to consider all opinions, and because of the inherent nature of large groups, they are unable to govern themselves anyway[65]. What used to be democratic 100 years ago is no longer democratic today, so only time will tell if these criticisms are properly dealt with in the future.

Although they like to, modern democracies cannot invoke the term universal suffrage. As explained previously, the term has changed dramatically over time. Switzerland, one of the most quoted examples of applied democratism, only started allowing women to vote in the 1970s—it took another two decades to fully establish this in all cantons. Additionally, without proper

---

65   *Burnham* (1943), 128f.

opposition parties in social democracies, the only resulting pseudo-opposition is from alleged *politically right* parties and cadidates, whose presence is laughable to every right person. The pseudo-right does advocate some liberal values, but so do other social democratic parties. Across all social democracies, the parliament will include at least a symbolic pseudo-liberal party, a party promoting ‹christian values›, and a party tending towards nationalism. In reality, all three are social democratic. Since a conservative is someone who wants to conserve something, even social democrats can easily be conservative.

The extreme political right, in the form of liberalism, and even the extreme political left, in the form of anarchism[66], slowly ceased to be represented in political parliaments when the first social democrats became powerful enough to hold the majority and were able to be part of any given parliament for multiple governing periods. Democracies inherently embody the anonymous and unaccountable collective. As such, they can never be an instrument for liberalism. They cannot be advocated by the liberal person, although his nature would also forbid him to achieve anything through violence and coercion. The promise of successfully joining together the systems of liberty and equality is futile since they are not compatible, unlike what popular opinion suggests[67]. Although many values of

---

66   *Somary* (1984/2010), 114.
67   *Schnellenbach* (2019), 374.

constitutionalism and liberalism have been misused to embellish the boring term of democracy, the reality shows that democratism only ever provided the voters with a welfare state and a chance to vote. All other values of democracy, such as human rights, freedom of association and opinion, separation of powers, or rule of law, are part of classical liberalism and constitutionalism. Social democracies, however, actively and openly limit liberal values in favor of compromises between two systems. People who believe that democracy equates freedom and provides the liberal values they are accustomed to must find themselves in a dangerous position. They are prone to being exploited by politicians who falsely attribute liberal values to social democracy.

Because social democracies do not want their system to be removed by democratic means, most social democracies require the political parties and their candidates to have no objections against democratism and all its democratically legitimized institutions. This ensures that serious liberal alternatives to the present status quo are fantastically hard to achieve in any social democracy. Especially since multiple generations have learned to become fully dependent on the state. To worsen the situation, after World War II, socialist eugenics and racism[68]—favored by everyone from social democrats to extreme socialists—were now also

---

68   *Fritze* (2012), 183f.

bestowed on the right, further defiling it and rendering political opposition into nothing more than a pipe dream. Most people today who think of themselves as politically right are simply confused, conservative social democrats with nationalistic tendencies who would gladly use the democratic government to pass policies and legislation that benefit them at the expense of others.

Especially in Germany and Austria, of those pseudo-right people, some cling to the conservative revolution, which is known for its hostility towards liberalism. In a large multinational study on attitudes towards the term ‹capitalism›, people from Germany, France, Great Britain, Brazil, Japan, Italy, and Austria who described themselves as distinctively right-wing had a more negative attitude towards 'capitalism', than those who described themselves as slightly right-wing. While distinctively right-wing people from the United States, Sweden, Chile, South Korea, Spain, and Switzerland really did have a more positive attitude towards the term[69]. As such, it appears that many of those who think of themselves as right-wing cannot be taken at face value and must be questioned further to clarify whether they are confused or genuine politically right.

Many NGOs and certain social democratic government agencies, especially after World War II, diligently fought against communism. For many, at least their financial

---

69   *Zitelmann* (2022), 340f.

livelihood depended on the more moderate form of socialism reigning supreme over the extreme form. The uncontested omnipotence of social democratism post-World War II in Western governments led to the movement becoming a baseline for political thought in those same countries. Anything goes, as long as it builds upon social democratism and its many principles and social institutions. Unfortunately, whenever the voice of reason is democratic, the resulting system cannot be reasonable on a large scale since mob rule is predetermined. Originally, the social democrats were against all forms of indirect taxation. They felt it hurt the low-income working population disproportionally, who had to use more of their income towards buying daily necessities than those with higher incomes.

Newer social democrats have no problem with indirect taxes, such as value-added taxes. On the other hand, they have always preferred a progressive system of taxation. Although one could allege that they disregard the fact that inflation and people's own productivity-related increases in monetary compensation will push people into higher brackets, the author suggests that this is not the case. After vehemently advocating progressive taxation since the beginning of their political movement, one can say for sure that they are well aware of the drawbacks or acknowledge them as an advantage. Although it cannot be generalized, the author does allege that many social democrats do have poor levels of financial literacy.

Unless one commits a logical fallacy, if person A earns one and pays one, while person B earns two but pays three, equality can never be achieved unless one believes that some people are more equal than others or more deserving of equality, thereby defeating the concept of equality. Logical fallacies are a staple of socialist thought and have been present ever since early attempts in Ancient Greece to instrumentalize the state for the benefit of certain interest groups.

Under progressive taxation, no two people are equal since the different tax brackets specifically represent different levels of taxation. The original idea of progressive taxation has never been to generate more government income, as a flat rate that taxes everyone from the first cent generates more income than a progressive system does. Ever since early social democratic radical tax reforms in Europe, the redistributive factor in taxation has started to overpower simple income generation. Tax legislation today is not measured by efficiency or comprehensibility. The most important factors are social effects on the population and their use as political control mechanisms.

Keeping citizens in line by trying to limit their incomes is still the most effective way for governments to ensure that most of their subordinates have trouble emancipating themselves; some people try to relativize this by suggesting that they still have a house and enough to eat, so it cannot be too bad. This is not a sound argument. Compared to the old socialists from the nineteenth century, the new socialists have learned that combining their powers on an international scale leads to more pleasing results than trying to struggle against current orders and competing socialists. For that reason, national socialism and scientific socialism, both seen as archaic and disruptive forms of socialism today, cannot be tolerated in the social democratic worldview.

This is why so many insults today revolve around calling the opposing party a national socialist or communist. Not as an objective description, but simply as defamatory name-calling or an *ad hominem* attack. All of these groups comprise tiny minorities in any given population, even though it is often alleged that they are figuratively hiding around every corner. Old socialists were more inclined to be radical but also much more militant towards other socialists, compared to today. Most socialists were distrustful of each other, as they did not only compete on a political level but also on a theoretical one.

Ultimately, only moderate social democrats were able to prevail on a large scale in Western countries and successfully bring their agenda into the twenty-first century, which is certainly the lesser evil compared to more extreme forms of socialism that could have reemerged. Although radical ideas have the potential to change the world dramatically, those changes rarely last long unless implemented in a more moderate form over a longer period of time. Although moderate, small changes do accumulate over time and may amount to a great deal of change. As *Kuehnelt-Leddihn* suggested decades ago, «Even a Louis XIV, autocrat, centralist, and breaker of many of the best traditions as he was, would hardly have ventured to exercise three prerogatives which "progressive democracies" have claimed and do claim without batting an eye: prohibition of alcoholic beverages, conscription, and an income tax involving annual economic "confession" to the State . . . not to mention "nationalization" which is a specious form of theft.»[70]

Many people today illogically cling to the concept of democracy or treat it like a substitute religion. That being said, the percentage of people trusting democracy is falling steadily[71], as is trust in government in most OECD countries[72]; both correlate with the increasing problems that social democracies face. The democratic worldview establishes that democratism is the end point of history and that no other system can ever come afterwards. The suffering created in the name of the people and in the name of democracy is enough to put it on par with religious conflicts of the past. When the rule of law—an accomplishment of denouncing the arbitrary divine right of kings—starts being impeded by the

---

70   *Kuehnelt-Leddihn* (1952), 281.
71   2023 Edelman Trust Barometer, 8–11.
72   *OECD Trust in government (indicator)* (2023).

arbitrary rule of the masses, one should become alert. After the partial defeat of communism, multiple events catapulted the world into a new era. Starting with the unification of Germany, which caused real wages in the country to stagnate and not increase for decades[73] and cost trillions of euro to unite the two parts of Germany[74]. This event alone set forth a series of events in the 1990s that made a stronger European Union a reality. Because Germany was now united, acting as a strong baseline in the center of Europe, and communism in Europe had been defeated, a strong social democratic European Union was now feasible. Celebrating the success of social democracy and the defeat of communism, the World Anti-Communist League changed its name to the World League for Freedom and Democracy to reflect the change in international politics.

After the Maastricht Treaty established the European Union and the EU later introduced the European Single Market and the European Economic Area, the groundwork for an international supranational framework was successfully established. The organization has had massive issues actually enforcing the treaty, resulting in the whole Union becoming fiscally unstable. Government debt reached previously unseen levels, and no one prosecuted the governments responsible. The economic disaster continued to unfold when the European Union established the European

---

73   *Brenke* (2009), 550-560.
74   BT WD 4 - 3000 – 033/18.

Central Bank and the euro. This was a terrible decision in foresight and hindsight that, to the dismay of most citizens in the northern and southern European Union, caused real wages to drop considerably or at least stagnate for several years, as the euro did no longer allow member countries to devalue their currencies. Of the EU countries that have adopted it, those that suffered from the euro the most are Belgium, Germany, Italy, Spain, Portugal, and Greece, in no specific order. The Eastern-European countries benefited the most from the euro, although some other Western countries did so as well. The countries that benefited from the euro the most are Luxembourg, the Netherlands, Austria, Ireland, Finland, Slovenia, Lithuania, Estonia, Latvia, and Slovakia, in no specific order[75]. Although datasets on wages in Cyprus and Malta are scarce due to the small size of the two countries, data from the EU directly[76] does suggest that the wages in Cyprus stagnated for years, with only little growth over 15 years, while the wages in Malta did increase somewhat more than in Cyprus over the same period.

Even though there are outliers, there exist two distinct groups. The southern-European countries were the clear losers from the beginning, while the eastern-European countries have profited the most from the euro in the short time frame that most of them have been in the EU. It becomes clear that the overarching goal is still to

---

75   *OECD* (2023).
76   *AMECO* (autumn 2022).

prevent communism from reemerging in eastern-European countries, even if it means doing so at the expense of other member countries in the EU. The ECB, allegedly a guarantor of a stable currency, ignores its competencies and directly finances states by buying state-issued bonds. This type of *ultra vires* behavior is the most evident at the ECB, out of all EU institutions.

The real GDP per capita in most Western EU member states has increased only somewhat since 2000, while that of East European countries has increased dramatically. Belgium, the Netherlands, Austria, Denmark, Germany, Finland, and the former member state, the United Kingdom, all experienced real GDP growth of a mere 20 to 25 percent. With Ireland's 132.662 percent GDP growth as an outlier, the South European countries experienced the lowest real growth in GDP, by far. Italy takes the last place, growing only by 2.880 percent during the period. As if this economic growth were not unbalanced enough already, the Eastern European member states experienced growth of 56.366 percent in Slovenia and up to 188.718 percent in Lithuania[77]. It is clear that the European Union is not an economic union of equals. As long as the European Union tries to unify its member states beyond legal measures, due to the economic disparaties, the European Single Market and the European Economic Area are in danger of collapsing, especially in regard to

---

77 Own calculations. *EUROSTAT* (2023).

the massive subsidies flowing to various EU countries. Especially without the subsidies in agriculture, fishing, and farming, those countries would otherwise be incapable of competing in the European Economic Area. Some people praise the legal system behind the EU. In that case, leaving the legal system in place while completely ridding the European Union of any economic authority, including its monopoly on currency, will prove necessary when the European Union is to be preserved long-term. If this does not happen, the European Union will not survive the financial devastation it is creating in the Western European countries; it will simply implode and wither away. Similarly, as seen in the European Union, its own primary law prevents the member states from being prosecuted whenever they disregard the EU primary law that regulates fiscal responsibility, effectively preventing the primary law from being enforced[78]. This also explains why many EU member states continue from one economic crisis to the next. It can only be hoped that this is addressed in the near future.

Apart from the European Union, the 1990s also saw the emergence of the World Trade Organization. International globalization on the scale seen today was certainly the magnum opus of the many NGOs involved

---

78   Consolidated version of the Treaty on the Functioning of the European Union - PART THREE: UNION POLICIES AND INTERNAL ACTIONS - *TITLE VIII: ECONOMIC AND MONETARY POLICY - Chapter 1: Economic policy - Article 126* (ex Article 104 TEC) in: OJ C 115, 9.5.2008, 99–102.

in establishing the globalized system we see nowadays. It is still uncertain whether NGOs will continue to globalize in the coming decades. Perhaps, without the strong influence of key twentieth-century figures who died in recent years, the world might see a resurgence in protectionism. The social democratic movement was able to thrive in the twentieth century precisely because hundreds of important NGOs formed large portions of it. The result was a tightly-knit web of influence that currently reaches from the United States to Japan.

The mere fact that states, corporations, financial institutions, and NGOs work together on such a large scale ensures that the average person in a democracy has little authority over policies compared to the established structures that formed in the last century. The main goal seems to be to assist multinational corporations and institutions in their operations. Globalization has ensured that they can enterprise, without being restricted by individual states and their legislation.

The trend towards superordinate organizations controlling large parts of national legislation for multiple states is accelerating. Although some people like to speculate about the chance of a one-world government, history shows that the Holy Roman Empire already established a similar structure with regard to harmonized legislation. As established by one of the key twentieth-century figures in NGOs, the global system of internationalist interconnected politics and economics was to be implemented under the leadership of the United States[79], which partly explains the continued hegemony of the US. This is not to be misunderstood as neocolonialism on behalf of the United States, but as a guiding power for the Western states. Because the world is seeing a tendency towards economic fragmentation and protectionism, the future role of the United States is uncertain. Calls for more protectionism do, however, severely inhibit foreign policy and the globalism that the NGOs of the twentieth century fought for. Many of the organizations offer a space for discussing foreign relations, international politics, interventionist policies, and economics. They saved social democratism in the twentieth century. Without the influence of corporations, many social democracies would have deteriorated even faster than they already have.

As governments became more powerful in the late nineteenth and early twentieth centuries, it was in the interest of corporations and other non-governmental organizations to take part in the new political system of social democracy that started to dominate First-World countries from then on. Not doing so would have meant being subjected to arbitrary decision-making in the name of the masses. Lobbyism was therefore built into social democratism from the very beginning, whether through officially registered lobbyists or NGOs that

---

79   *Rockefeller* (2003), 406.

organize meetings to discuss important issues. Social democratism is completely in line with corporatism, as seen in the prevalence of subsidies and protective legislation.

The recent decades of international Western peace have been possible, in large part, thanks to these same NGOs. As the post-World War II power structures start to crumble, the frequency and gravity of economic disasters must necessarily increase. Although some social democratic governments are trying to forcefully transition into a green, degrowth economy, it is unlikely that oil will be completely banned in the next few decades since many large oil companies are owned partially or fully by states[80].

Few states would dare to eliminate their own stake in the industry simply to please those factions who see renewable energy as a viable alternative to the current primary energy sources. Many other authors have written in depth about the fallacies of renewable energies, especially in conjunction with economic planning, so this will not be elaborated further. Although the role of oil has decreased in the past few decades, it has been responsible for large portions of the economic growth in the nineteenth and twentieth centuries. In the twentieth century, most of the First-World countries peaked in their consumption of oil by the 1970s, which led to the oil crisis in the same decade. Emerging

---

80   *Yergin* (1990/2009), 770.

economies in Third- and Second-World countries will use a lot more oil and coal in the coming decades, while the First-World countries will inevitably transition to other means of energy production over time. The forced transition to renewable energy by the state will potentially set back their economies by decades and decrease the standard of living since companies will be unable to manage their businesses economically, which results in decreased competitiveness. Robotics, combined with machine learning and artificial intelligence, will obviously play a larger role in the coming decades. This means that artificially limiting energy capabilities is especially problematic in this environment of demographic change. One that requires large amounts of stable energy, capital, and money to complete the transition from the service sector economy to a fully automated one.

The international social democratic utopia may be coming to an end in the twenty-first century. Few governments still have a firm financial foundation, with many of them being kept from bankruptcy only because of constant inflation and debt that their subordinates must pay for indefinitely. The modern social institutions are stuck in the past, and their operation is unsustainable. As artificial intelligence and robotics become more salient topics in the twenty-first century, social democracies are too stagnant and inflexible to handle the massive shift in employment and loss of revenue. How social democracies address this change is yet to be seen. Finding a sensible way of allowing people to coexist with governments and NGOs without either of the two parties having too much influence on the population seems most important in the mean time. An alternative system will be described in the last chapter that is dynamic and flexible enough to deal with the problems of the twenty-first century.

RECAP

- Social democratism is a mild form of socialism.
- The system has enjoyed world-wide primacy in most First-World countries since at least World War II.
- Social democracies continue to exist because of compromises between radical socialism and liberalism.
- There exists little to no true opposition in social democracies.
- Voting does not legitimize.
- Social democratism competes with radical forms of socialism.
- The twenty-first century presents problems too difficult to solve for the ideology of social democratism.
- NGOs influence the status quo more than anything.

5. LAW AS INSTRUMENTUM REGNI

When referring to property in this book, the author is referring to the concept of *proprietas* in the Ancient Roman law. Unfortunately, the modern english language has no satisfactory term to distinguish between *proprietas* and *possessio*. The *proprietas* is the legal authority over something, while the *possessio* is the authority to physically possess something. Someone who has the authority to physically possess something might not have legal authority over that thing. The relationship between landlord and renter is an example to illustrate this concept.

Laws, morals, culture, and traditions are what make civilization possible. They cannot be forcefully changed by any authority; they can only be diluted and subverted. Even though no single person has the same values, most people who live among each other in groups share a similar culture and traditions. Through these, they can generally be identified by other groups. Because of these inherent differences, humans differentiate between countries. Although nothing can be universally attributed to a whole population, since people do differ from cultural norms, every culture has established its own set of overarching characteristics that the majority of people in that population live by. These values are further reinforced through family and friends, who themselves are reinforced in their behavior by others. It appears that humans are unable to live without simple rules[81]. Because humans are not rational angels, every group needs rules to live by.

NATURAL LAW AND LEGAL POSITIVISM

Even liberalism needs an overarching set of rules, since the absence of simple rules causes the individual to recede and the underlying person to start degrading into its animalistic form. Liberalism is an ideology that embodies the constant control of the government, natural law is the only set of rules that could ever adhere to the strict concept of limited government. Because the governed need to be protected from the government, natural law itself does not adhere to legal positivism; it cannot be created by legislation and is only found through reason, logic, in nature, and in human behavior. Law that is inalienable and protects life, liberty, and property[82] must be the basis of every equitable legal system. At least if one wishes to accept the concept of inalienable human rights. These fundamental concepts ensure that large-scale human culture can not only exist but thrive to its best ability. If liberalism were widespread, constitutions would not be needed since

81   *Burlamaqui/Nugent (transl.)/Korkman (ed.) (1752/2006)*, 64.
82   *Locke (1689/1884)*, 234f.

everyone knew their natural, inalienable rights. In other words, if people instinctively saw harmful acts against others as being horrible, there would be no need for an artificial institution[83]. However, because humans are not completely rational, this remains nothing more than a theoretical wish. Liberalism, unlike anarchism, accepts this human flaw and tries to work with it. Although one might be led to believe that legal positivism could be an adequate correction mechanism, this is not the case. Liberalism, personified by the rule of law, does not allow the individual to be subordinated to legislation. After all, no one wishes for the rule of legislation, but the rule of law. Because legislation is inherently positivist, it must be accepted as legal primate, and subordinate even natural law. To question the legitimacy of allegedly democratically legitimized legislation must then be on par with questioning political intelligence. In legal positivism, legislation allegedly originates in a complicated process of weighing up different opinions and regarding the situation of all involved and affected persons to eventually come up with an enlightened, equitable, and handcrafted piece of legislation.

Legal positivism, therefore, does not act in accordance with liberalism. Such a liberal legal system should be concerned with upholding minimal legislation; the majority of legal effort should go towards the interpretation of natural law and how it affects

---

83   *de Molinari* (1849), 278.

individual situations. Such a constitution, based on natural law, should merely have marginal amounts of legislation to clarify the meaning of natural rights. Natural rights are both liberty rights and claim rights. The right to life creates the necessity of respecting another person's life. On the same note, a person has a claim against everyone to force them to respect his life. All forms of socialism, on the other hand, will never allow natural law to enter their legal realm since it acts as the only proper correction mechanism for unjust legislation. *Locke* establishes that natural law stands as an eternal rule for men, legislators, and others[84]. According to his view, humans tend to give up some of their freedom to the state to protect their lives, liberty, and property.

They do this because the whole society, personified by the state, can penalize breaches of natural law more effectively than individuals in nature ever could. Legislation is therefore used not to control and oppress people or regulate their property but to prevent others from breaching natural law. As this is fundamental to understanding the ideology of liberalism, this liberal understanding of natural law will become the basis of this chapter. An inherent problem of natural law is that the old liberal doctrine did not conceptualize a world where people would be unreasonable and subscribe to the radical doctrines of the French Revolution as well as

---

84   *Locke* (1689/1884), 261f.

those in the nineteenth and twentieth centuries[85]. Finding one's way back to liberal reasoning seems like an impossible task today, in a world of intertwined social institutions, but might be the only option once the current social democracies fall victim to their own decadence.

Natural law differentiates between law and legislation, while the prevailing legal positivism conflates the two terms since it establishes that there must not exist any form of correction mechanism except for inadequate legal positivist dogma. The legislator is typically infallible—until he is, and the legislation has to be corrected afterwards. Natural law prevents inequitable legislation from occurring in the first place. The liberal constant of natural law in the ideology of socialism is the state. In liberalism, nothing can go against the law, while in socialism, nothing can go against the authority of the state. In different terms, while in liberalism natural law can be used to protect oneself from the state, in socialism the state cannot use natural law to protect itself from its citizens. Therefore, it must try to subordinate it or at least hollow it out. The state can freely change legislation, removing the permanence of law that is so crucial to keeping peace and predictability in a civilization. In social democracies, the judge can sometimes slightly divert from legislation to match individual cases, which gives him more leeway

---

85   *von Mises* (1949/2020), 861.

compared to the archaic Roman *ius strictum*, which does not allow for any deviation in interpretation.

On the other hand, the legislation under extreme forms of socialism is always absolute. Everyone is subjected to the enlightened fabrication of the legislators, who want to create and form a superior human based on their ideology, completely disregarding the negative effects this has on the population. As modern social democracies age, a specific pattern becomes apparent. The noticeable shift away from customary and hereditary law. Instead, legislators come up with new legislation based on opinions and the limited experience and expertise of government ministries or similar affiliated legislative bodies and institutions. Especially tax legislation, which has become harder to understand and only benefits two groups.

Those who earn a living trying to think of new tax planning strategies, and, of course, the government. The more nebulous, contradictory, and confusing the legislation is, the more lucrative it becomes for those two groups. No matter which social democracy one wants to examine today, they all have overly long and complicated tax legislation that guarantees that no single person can claim to have a particularly grounded understanding of the whole tax legislation. Only larger tax accounting firms have the luxury to fully penetrate the hard shell of tax legislation. It is still open to discussion how those firms and even the state will deal with artificial general intelligence, which could lead to more widespread usage and misuse of tax planning models in the near future.

Although modern legislation is mostly based on having claims against others, Ancient Rome mixed procedural and substantive legislation and ended up with a system that did not differentiate between the judge's decision on the case and the real substantive legal situation[86]. All legislation should be abstract and affect an undetermined number of people, so individual groups are not given any preference over others. Sadly, especially in tax legislation and when subsidizing, the legislature seems to forget all about those principles, resulting in legislation that favors special interest groups. To give an example, the freedom to pursue any business or economic activity is a staple claim that all social democracies adhere to. In reality, the freedom to enterprise is nothing more than a sham. In order to open a medical practice, a law firm, a company supplying power, etc., there are countless rules, legislation, compulsory education and training, and licenses to go through, all to protect those already in business from competition. This is no different than the guilds in the Middle Ages, with the main difference being that those never claimed to guarantee any freedom to pursue a business.

---

86   *Wesel* (2022), 182.

CONSTRAINING POWER

For the mean person living under a social democratic government, the constitution might appear to be the only tangible document that can limit the state's power. To allow state judges to deviate from the constitution is a grave encroachment on all civil liberties still left under democratic governments. As time passes and legislation becomes more conflicting and complex, these encroachments must occur more frequently. Social democratism will have to turn more towards extremism if it wishes to retain its core. When law is reduced to positivist legislation and becomes a tool for governments to shape their citizens, the rule of law becomes nothing more than an alien concept. This is a critical weakness in social democracies and one of the reasons for their downfall in this century. The term legal usually describes something that the mean population agrees to be equitable, while illegal is the opposite. People do not think poorly of theft because it is illegal; instead, theft is illegal because people think poorly of it.

This principle is endangered by positivist legislation since it can easily corrupt this understanding of what is legal and illegal and good or bad when certain interest groups and voter blocks are favored or disfavored by legislators. Legislation created by singular and subjective opinions that conform the population to the legislation is not equitable. To favor legislation that conforms itself to the population seems much more reasonable. Natural law achieves this by reducing all human wants and needs to a few easily understandable, inalienable rights. The mean population will agree on those values, since none of them disadvantage anyone or favor specific groups and behaviors. It is convincing that there is no other correction mechanism available that could substitute natural law without compromising the law itself and turning into more legislation. The correction mechanism cannot be more of the same. Even constitutions only provide protection *de jure* because written text alone does not prevent states from assuming more power.

Constitutions of totalitarian regimes either provide weak protection from the state or do so on such a superficial level that they can easily be relativized by judges whenever special circumstances require special actions and exceptions. Under liberal governments, constitutions can never be relativized or interpreted to the disadvantage of the citizen, since this alone entirely defeats the purpose of a constitution based on natural law. Strong constitutions favor governments that remain stable and limited in power over time. The stronger a constitution is, the more it provides reasons for those in power not to change it due to personal interest[87]. Weak constitutions favor governments that accumulate power and then decline and disintegrate over time. As such, having a strong constitution is of the utmost importance

---

87   *Constant/Hofmann (ed.)/O`Keeffe (transl.)* (1815/1980/2003), 96.

to a government's longevity and stability. In the future, artificial superintelligence could reasonably enforce constitutions without any human interference. Although change can be positive, excessive change often leads to instability. When the state has the authority to regulate without natural law as a correction mechanism in mind, planning ahead seems more like a game of chance. On the other hand, regulation is indispensable for aligning the collective with the policies and ideas of the government. No socialist state was ever able to, nor will it ever align the entire population with its values, since all forms of socialism violate fundamental natural rights. Some people will always be opposed to such a system; as such, only force, coercion, and group dynamics can ensure that most people act contrary to their natural values and morals.

No matter what political system the people of a population are subjected to, in all of them there is some form of legislation present, whether that is written or spoken legislation. There is no way around legislation, as it creates the option to plan ahead, no matter how basic the civilization or legislation is. At its most basic concept, legislation can support and complement natural law. It can also supplement customary law, such as the *lex mercatoria* of the Middle Ages, which appears to have been an overarching set of laws created by European traders and merchants to facilitate trade, similar to modern commercial legislation. In its most overarching form, legislation removes natural law altogether. Even though judges adhering to legal positivism can still correct positivist legislation, this does not provide a satisfactory correction mechanism.

Further legislation, beyond natural law, should conform to natural law and the population, not the other way around. When legislation is politicized by ideologies, the end goal will always justify the means necessary. Often, the socialist ‹greater good› is used as an excuse. The greater good is measured using a deluded form of subjective utilitarianism, in which the political actors selectively reduce or increase the importance of certain values to fit the political ideology. The field of jurisprudence is presented with the legislation in its normative sense[88]. Its job is not to create new forms of legislation; instead, it wants to understand the meaning of the legal norms and provide different legal interpretations as a result of interacting with the legislation. Every single type of legislation must be laid out and interpreted. It does not matter how clear or evident a piece of legislation is; it must be interpreted. Similarly, all contracts between parties must also be laid out and interpreted, since even a transparent and unproblematic contract can manifest different interpretations of the same situation. As such, each interpretation depends on hermeneutically significant circumstances[89], meaning that different people will fabricate different interpretations. But even judicial

---

88   *Larenz/Canaris* (1995), 25.
89   *Larenz/Canaris* (1995), 28.

cases must be interpreted, since they are part of the state and, at least indirectly, affect the applicability of positivist legislation. When the main reason for new legislation lies in molding the population to fit an ideology, it is no longer just. Of course, this problem only persists when humans, with their ideologically loaded emotions, have authority to legislate against natural law. Humans are incapable of objective legislation beyond observing their natural rights. Any attempt to prove otherwise will only result in some people being advantaged at the expense of others.

The more legislation exists, the less understandable it becomes for the layman, whether that is a natural person or a legal person. At some point, it becomes too much even for jurists to handle. This results in the extreme compartmentalization of jurisprudence. Unlike in the medical professions, specialization in law-related professions is not a sign of progress. Even many centuries ago, there was a realization that official records of property could lead to fewer lawsuits because multiple people could no longer claim to be the owners of the same property. This would, in turn, cause fewer lawyers to be necessary[90] to deal with such problems. It appears that it is in the interest of everyone to prevent lawsuits whenever possible. But not just the number of lawsuits is problematic. The intransparency of legislation is what creates the necessity for more

---

90   *Petty* (1662), 9f.

lawyers than ever. In all modern social democracies, especially in the important legal jurisdictions of the United States and the United Kingdom, the number of jurists has increased disproportionately to the population. Larger numbers of jurists are not a good sign, since more lawyers must then compete against others for the same number of cases available. Although competition is always good for the consumer, the layperson sees the lawyer as an inherent specialist. In reality, there exist large qualitative differences in legal competence between lawyers.

The problem in modern social democracies is that parliaments (congress in the US) often meet multiple times a week to discuss and pass legislation. Not only is it impossible for a single person to read and comprehend that much legislation, but the fact that the frequency of legislation increases must lead to a decrease in objective legislative quality. In addition, most of the representatives responsible for passing it are not qualified and are unable to understand it beyond a superficial level, simply because legislation today typically requires special knowledge of other fields of practice. In the Holy Roman Empire of the German Nation, the parliament met only when it was specifically necessary. Usually once every one to three years. Before the meeting, the electors were given six months to prepare for the meeting[91]. This ensured that the electors

---

91   *Freiherr von Pufendorf/Breslau* (1667/1870), 92f.

had enough time to understand the legislation, and the legislation written had a standard of quality that is completely missing from its modern equivalent. Another problematic issue seen in most governments, both current and historic, is that most operate under their own dedicated legislation and rules. Although it is alleged that status and class privileges no longer exist, the government, parliaments, certain organizations, ambassadors, diplomats, and diplomatic-like persons all have privileges ranging from full political immunity to exemption from national law to not being subjected to taxation. Even though this violates the principle of equality before the law, there are numerous breaches of a similar nature in the legislation of social democracies today.

Although it is commonly assumed that political classes of significance no longer exist nowadays, there are still numerous entities and persons that have a higher or lower position than others. How that can constitute equality is truly a mystery, without extensive mental gymnastics. Natural law, on the other hand, retains objectivity and does not discriminate. Those wanting different legislation and liability for states continue to elude a false sense of moral superiority that tends to eminate from public policy graduates and those who favor cameralist accounting. Until the mean population understands that no economic actor—not even the state—can be subject to favorable rules in a market, the constant crises in the name of the common good will become more extreme as time passes. Since the individual person cannot infringe the life, liberty, or property of other individuals without being punished, so must the state be punished if it infringes the life, liberty, or property of its citizens.

History suggests on many occasions that people in positions of power will eventually take advantage of their position somehow. Because of this simple observation, democracies separate government powers —at least in theory. In practice, this does not work, since fully separating powers is impossible when they are still deeply intertwined and dependent on each other. As such, independent branches of government are a myth. Artificial superintelligence appears to be a sensible and viable alternative in the future, especially for political systems that pride themselves on the separation of powers. Even today, some states openly breach this important principle[92][93], usually without any concequence. Although Great Britain managed to greatly reduce the power the Lord High Chancellor of Great Britain previously held, problems of separation of powers have not been fully resolved yet. The European Union is a legal disaster in terms of separation of powers. The Court of Justice of the European Union decides against the EU in so few cases that it is unlikely, and unrealistic, that there exists realistic control of the EU commission and parliament. The EU commission also

92   *Lüdemann* (2015), 69, 77, 82.
93   *Hochschild* (2022), 26.

takes advantage of the parliament's powers regularly. In the United States, the Attorney General is still elected by the president, who, as part of the executive, is electing the head of the judicial system—someone who is supposed to keep the government in check. Similar problems, although arguably worse, can be seen in Germany[94] and Austria, where the Minister of Justice, who is also elected by the executive, is responsible for electing judges and deciding whether they get promoted.

He is also authorized to give them orders. Complaints of the German judges' association have not been taken seriously ever since the inception of the Federal Republic of Germany, since the practice of the minister having authority over judges has been present in previous iterations of Germany as well. It does not have to be elaborated on why this is a terrifying situation for anyone who values separation of powers, especially in regard to Germany's history of judges conforming to the state. The separation of powers is also breached by the mere fact that the majority parliaments in social democracies cannot effectively control the government since it hasdirect ties to the same people who comprise the parliament. Only a parliament that has no ties to the government could actively control it and keep it in check. This also means that it is more equitable to have a monarch by birth who is controlled by a parliament of

---

94   Judgement of the Court (Grand Chamber) of 27 May 2019, *Minister for Justice and Equality v OG and PI,* C-508/18 and C-82/19 PPU, EU:C:2019:456, paragraph 80 and 88.

unaffiliated, neutral, and qualified people who gain nothing when deciding in favor of the government. When the parliament becomes affiliated with the very person or government it is supposed to control, defending democratic values becomes nothing more than a play on words, imposed by those who benefit from the situation. Once the state is given more power, it never voluntarily gives it up again. Constitutions therefore must limit state power, since giving up power is harder than not having it to begin with. Usually, the state uses times of crisis to facilitate more power, which includes the power to increase tax rates. These surges in power are then guaranteed to be temporary. Only after the crisis will one realize that the state has gotten used to its new power and will not give it up without equally severe measures forcing it to reduce it.

Since even criticizing alleged democratic values is seen as heresy by many ideologically deluded or uneducated people, it becomes even easier for the state to breach the separation of powers in the open and simply proclaim it to be a new form of democracy worthy of protection. Voting does not legitimize anyone if the alternative is that politicians get elected anyway. One should wonder why there is no option on the voting ballot to prevent any parliament from forming. *Leoni* establishes that, unlike supply and demand in the market, winners and losers in elections are neither complementary nor compatible with each other[95]. This commonly results in childish and senseless political discussions in regard to which party is the best—not realizing that all of them are merely different sides of the same coin. Democratic participation in modern nation-states is not about having a say in the government or being represented, for that matter. Voting in democracies is all about deciding the living situation of other people with the help of the government—all in good Rousseauian fashion. Due to artificial intelligence, advanced computing, and radical technological changes within this century, humans might be incapable of understanding the world that they live in, in the near future. Using artificial superintelligence in place of the fully human state seems to be the only future-proof and realistic option in the twenty-first century and beyond. Although this sounds unlikely for most people living today, this is a definite probability. It can be achieved by aligning artificial intelligence with the ideas of natural law, because it is still unknown whether artificial superintelligence could create its own concepts of law when being applied in such situations. Computational legal theory will research and start applying more of these currently abstract concepts.

---

95   *Leoni/Kemp (ed.)* (1961/1991), 236.

Recap

- Natural law comprises the right to life, liberty, and property.
- Legislation should not be conflated with law, and vice versa.
- Legal positivism is not compatible with natural law, and vice versa.
- Social democracies must adhere to stronger constitutions in the future to prevent the state from usurping too much power.
- There exists a natural need for a state, since not all humans behave rationally enough to be able to uphold a modern civilization without a state.
- State liability, including subjecting the state to the same civil legislation, is imperative if one believes in the rule of law.

6. Taxation: the Road to Redistribution

Short history of taxation

The word taxation etymologically comes from the Latin word *taxare* and means to evaluate or assess something or someone. The second meaning is to charge someone with something. Historically, many governments assessed the population's possessions and then imposed a certain charge on them. This charge was not always due in monetary form and varied from government to government. Grain, livestock, and everything else imaginable were collected. Monetary charges were not common in early governments and were usually levied only temporarily, for purposes of war or religious celebration. Early governments tried to legitimize taxation because the government protected the population from outsiders. In early cultures, taxes and other duties were also seen as a form of religious worship, since the ruler was typically alleged to have a tight bond with the gods and would, in turn, offer the gods sacrifices to appease and soothe them.

Similarly to early governments, the rulers in the Middle

Ages tried to legitimize taxation because they thought of their position as God-given. This was part of their feudalist worldview, in which it was morally right to have peasants pay a certain amount of money or resources in exchange for being able to cultivate and live on the land and receive protection in times of distress and conflict. Because of the gradual shift to a monetary economy in the late Middle Ages, monetary forms of taxation were becoming more common. They were typically levied in absolute numbers, usually in the form of a head tax or a fixed amount on the land the peasants were given to live on. Historically, a fixed head tax provided diminishing returns for the governments, as the government-issued currencies frequently devalued over time and the fixed tax needed to be constantly readjusted as a result. Other times, the ruler would invent different taxes that were typically levied for a short while until the goal associated with the tax was met. For instance, when fighting a war, the ruler might have levied an additional tax if he could not finance the war through his own efforts.

Historically, the aristocracy, state employees, and religious institutions were not taxed—even until recent centuries. Today, those with the necessary means also have no business paying taxes. For the longest time, taxation was a fate purely attributed to the lowest class, which mostly consisted of peasants. The clergy in the Middle Ages, despite not being part of the state, also demanded a part of the peasants' harvest yield for alleged religious purposes. The nobility of that time did not have to create or support a massive number of government institutions, departments, and offices. Therefore, those governments were able to be upheld with a fraction of what modern social democracies require when upholding their own status quo.

After the Industrial Revolution allowed for previously unprecedented wealth to be created, the emerging middle class was subjected to taxation as well. After the liberation of the peasants and farmers in the nineteenth century, some of these taxes were abolished, and others later followed after the revolutions of 1848 and the decades that followed. These forced payments, levied by the aristocracy, were abolished but were being continued by the new institutionalized governments of Europe. Churches, the aristocracy, and the state were still exempt from taxation in most parts of the continent. Compared to modern tax rates, the taxes were unbelievably low. Even so, by the majority of people in those days, the low single-digit tax rates were deemed too high. The population in those times was fed up, and some openly beat up tax collectors on the streets.

Those supporting the revolutions of 1848 demanded a somewhat isonomic parliament of representative politicians who were supposed to decide on behalf of the voters and represent the population and their interests. The revolutions failed, and taxation and government spending continued without true representation. In the last quarter of the nineteenth century, socialists and social democrats began to have more influence in European parliaments but were mostly overshadowed by other political parties. The majority of people living in the last quarter of the nineteenth century experienced a drastic rise in living conditions compared to the early nineteenth century and especially previous centuries. Using the state as a tool was still a foreign concept to most people. The socialist politicians already sensed that the government would play a more important role in the future. This, of course, increased not only the cost of operation but also the influence of the government on its population. In 1881, *Adolf Wagner,* a socialist economist and Prussian politician, believed that the government should not only finance social programs through social politics but also directly intervene in economies. Not just through heavy taxation to limit income but by directly intervening because of discrepancies in incomes[96]. *Wagner* was certainly not the first to think of a progressive income tax.

INCOME TAX

There had been previous attempts in Prussia in the early nineteenth century. Although Ancient Rome already had a wealth tax, the modern income tax, in its progressive nature, is an idea deeply embedded in the ideology of cameralism. The seventeenth and eighteenth centuries

---

96   *Sahm* (2018), 252.

brought us the first ideas of a progressive income tax, put forward by cameralists such as *Caspar Klock* and *Johann Heinrich Gottlob von Justi* and socialist thinkers such as *Russeau*[97]. The gravity of those ideas can still be felt today. Although not progressive in nature, the dixième, established in the royal decree of October 10th 1710, by Louis XIV, was a flat income tax, similar to the tenth of the Middle Ages, meant to be levied temporarily during times of war. In later decades, up until the French Revolution, the tax was reintroduced a number of times under the name of vingtième[98], which now constituted five percent instead of the previous ten.

Unlike the original dixième, the latter form of the tax allowed large portions of the First and Second Estates to become exempt from the tax, which led the protesters of the French Revolution to abolish the tax. The revolution marked another chapter in the road to a progressive income tax. The result of the revolution was that the revolutionists demanded a progressive income tax. Soon afterwards, the British *William Pitt* followed with an income tax in 1799 to prevent the insolvency of the British government during the Napoleonic Wars[99]. It was levied only temporarily in Britain but was later reintroduced in the first half of the 19th century. Other states followed in the late 19th century, including Sweden, the United States, Italy, Japan, the Netherlands,

---

97   *Sahm* (2023), 4.
98   *Willis* (December 1895), 37f.
99   *Auerbach* (1987), 1.

New Zealand, and Norway[100], but the tax itself stayed largely similar to the British model. The second-most important income tax innovation in the First World of the 19th century were the Prussian income tax reforms. In the 1890s, former communist and Prussian finance minister *Johannes von Miquel* created the blueprint for the modern progressive income tax as it is known today. Although the tax rates were still all in the low single digits, large portions of the population opposed the tax. At the same time, it was becoming more feasible to increase taxes, unlike in the early nineteenth century, when the monetary economy was not yet as established[101].

Miquel was one of the first to completely base the tax system around people declaring their own income instead of having it estimated by the state. This, in turn, had previously been criticized because the tax collectors would enter the houses and apartments on occasion to assess the taxable goods and income. Although the new income tax was less of an encroachment on the civil liberties of the population, the new change in self-assessment made the act of paying taxes so much more complicated for the average citizen. As such, the profession of the tax advisor slowly started being established in the coming decades and soon became a global and staple aspect of the enforcement of tax legislation in all social democracies. The new tax system

---

100   *Genovese/Scheve/Stasavage* (2016).
101   *Ullmann* (2005), 50.

did fix the problems of the old tax systems in Europe. Those were even more inefficient than the new system because they mostly relied on mass compliance without strict enforcement, did not cover all sources of income, favored specific classes, or levied a plethora of different and constantly changing taxes. The temporary nature of taxes, however, soon began to fade with the widespread adoption of the income tax. As the Industrial Revolution created new and previously unseen forms of income, trying to assess and tax individual types of income proved to be ineffective, so the general income tax was deemed to be a more appropriate solution to the problem. That being said, the government of the United States, for decades, did not levy an income tax. Only during and after World War I did social democratic governments start raising rates substantially[102]. Times of war and distress have historically been the times during which governments raise marginal tax rates. The tax rates during the war then become the new standard. Implementing higher tax rates is easier when people are desensitized to higher tax rates, especially after experiencing a war economy.

In most modern governments, the income tax soon became a staple tax in their financial system—the revenue from the tax continued to comprise larger amounts of total state revenue. As the tax matured under the various governments, it soon became a

---

102 *Piketty/Goldhammer (transl.) (2014), 499.*

general income tax, covering all types of income. Punishment for evasion became more severe, and the tax was no longer tied to a specific purpose. The income tax was now universally justified by its means—the means of redistribution. As long as the goal was politically feasible, new taxes were no longer seen as illegitimate. That being said, even during the nineteenth century, the idea of a morally justified income tax was already being discarded.

Heinrich Ludwig Biersack suggests that it is especially reprehensible when the socialist or communist purpose of slowly working towards abolishing the status quo of property is the basis for the tax. Instead, he suggests a system of indirect taxes and usage fees that directly correspond to specific state functions[103]. The overwhelming majority in the literature, however, did welcome the tax. This opened entirely new options for social democrats to increase their power with the assistance of social institutions. The aspects of financing the government's day-to-day operations and defending the country and its citizens in times of distress and conflict faded into unimportance. It was now of secondary concern because many governments started becoming acquainted with the comfort of large amounts of debt after World War I. The state had become the guarantor of equality and well-being. Since then, the rule of law has devolved into a nuissance when evaluating

---

103   *Biersack* (1850), 98.

whether legislation is just and equitable enough to balance the interests of different parties and discouraging alleged unjust behavior, also known as asocial in other forms of socialism.

The late nineteenth century also introduced many people to the first proper government safety net. *Otto von Bismarck,* the conservative chancellor of the German Reich at the time, was the one who passed legislation against social democratism, communism, and other forms of socialism[104]; he also passed legislation that established forced government insurance against accidents, invalidity, illnesses, and old age. His goal was to extinguish the ideology of social democratism by appeasing social democratic voters with socialist reform ideas and alienating them from the social democratic parties. Unknowingly, he created the basis for many modern social democratic institutions. He later lost the subsequent elections to the social democrats and retired from his political career. Governments in the early twentieth century typically tried to focus on a few taxes and, for that reason, levied those much higher than when they had multiple small taxes and duties. Nowadays, social democratic governments have both. High tax rates and a large quantity of constantly changing taxes. This results in an intransparent system of tax legislation as the employees in the state ministries try to keep up with creating new and modifying old

---

104   Gesetz gegen die gemeingefährlichen Bestrebungen der Sozialdemokratie vom 21. Oktober 1878 (RGBl. S. 351).

taxes to match the newest definition and interpretation of the term social.

Building on *Johannes von Miquel's* tax law, the legislation passed by Weimar Republic finance minister *Matthias Erzberger,* who was a prominent advocate of taxation as a means of redistributing wealth on a large scale, further increased the tax burden on the population. The marginal tax rate increased from 4 percent to 60 percent[105], under *Erzberger,* which led to an increase in tax evasion, while complaints about high taxation and hyperinflation became louder and more frequent. He left his role as finance minister in 1920 and was murdered a year later. The hyperinflation of the 1920s, also created by politicians, destroyed all savings and left a large portion of the population dependent on the government. Inflation discourages saving and investing because the return may be completely wiped out by it. This makes people dependent on government safety nets, which is further encouraged by social democratic ideology.

PROBLEMS OF MODERN TAXATION

It is obvious that despite widespread use of technology and higher productivity than in previous centuries, the process of paying taxes is becoming more complicated. This should seem strange, especially when taking into account that state revenue from taxes has grown by

---

105   *Hirschburger (ed.)* (1923), 185.

fantastically incredible amounts in the last few decades, all around the world, disproportionally to the population increase. States have more revenue to spend on qualitatively higher legislation, yet the new legislation becomes harder to understand, even for legal professionals, while the mean population is expected to routinely spend money and time on accountants, advisors, and lawyers, or deal with the massive headache of not understanding what must seem like a legal parrallel universe they live in. Especially tax legislation must become more complicated in social democracies. This happens by design because the act of levying taxes in a social democracy must also always fulfill social functions, mostly with the goal of changing and influencing certain behaviors in the population.

The fact that many people have to spend excruciating time every single year to assess their tax payment to the state will never change, unless fiscal concerns become the only reason for taxation again. The overarching ideology of social democratism and behavioral control in modern tax legislation greatly contributes to the problem of tax reforms. Simple solutions would obviously affect firms, which live off complicated tax legislation. In addition, the many calls for legislation reforms all fail to realize that reforming the tax legislation would rid social democracies of a large amount of oppression potential. It is part of their political leverage and will be reformed only as a last resort if the ideology is close to collapsing. This explains why there has not been a single worthwhile major reform of tax legislation in the established social democracies. In every social democracy, the act of paying taxes is still complicated, and the tax legislation continues to be intransparent.

The progressive tax systems of social democracies function completely on their own without the need to raise the present tax rates because percentages are used to levy the taxes, which are inherently relative. The governments are sure to receive more income with each passing year, unless an extreme economic correction occurs. Even inflation increases the tax burden on the population since it leads to nominal increases in wages and automatically puts people into higher tax brackets. After World War I, the idea that there exists a maximum amount of profit that is socially acceptable led to the perceived social democratic necessity of funneling the surplus profit into the government, which then proceeded to redistribute the money. The reason private savings are not promoted and heavily inhibited goes back to the social democratic theory that accumulation of wealth in a few hands is bad—except in the hands of the government, which acts as the great equalizer—and therefore should artificially be kept low through taxation and intervention in the economy.

This is completely in line with current trends and makes sense if one remembers that social democratism is a form of socialism. Low-income earners are taxed little and therefore still have good chances of increasing their income until they inevitably land in the higher brackets themselves. Few states increase their progressive tax rates proportionally to inflation; even fewer have done this since the inception of their progressive taxes, but no state also increases them with respect to real economic growth. Flat taxes do not have the problem of keeping up with arbitrary brackets because they never change. They are also more equal, as they affect everyone equally, no matter their income or economic situation.

Percentages are already relative. Taking a flat tax rate of ten percent as an example, someone who earns 100 times as much also pays 100 times the absolute amount in taxes. For financially illiterate social democrats, this is not sufficient to artificially keep the living standard low enough to ensure most people are unable to save and invest money on their own and have to rely on the collective welfare state. Their skewed view of equality operates entirely against logic. Keep in mind that the goal of progressive taxation is to gradually bring everyone to the same level of income by reducing the income of one person to supplement that of another. Instead of letting people become wealthier on their own, the government tries to assimilate the wealthy with the poor. If everyone is poorer, people are more equal than if they rise from being poor into the middle class and from the middle class into the upper class. For that reason alone, greater standards of living will always create more inequality initially, until the poor, who lag behind temporarily, follow by becoming more productive themselves. Ever since the Industrial Revolution, most countries have experienced a drastic increase in living standards, while the number of people in poverty has declined dramatically[106]. An environment of progressive taxation explicitly hinders the growth of middle-class incomes because their real wages are subjected to the most severe tax increases. Once the taxpayer has reached the highest bracket, mandatory central bank inflation targets ensure that he never drops below his current tax rate, unless he loses his primary source of income.

The progression in a progressive tax system also disincentivizes low-income earners to earn more, since they realize they will pay more taxes disproportionally on their real income increase. Although many social democracies had much higher maximum tax rates in the past, few people reached the higher brackets compared to today. In addition, options for deductions were much more plentiful in the past. As the government decides to increase its revenue, getting rid of deductions is the easiest way to ensure higher revenue, especially in the long term when certain deductions are being used disproportionately more than others. The system of deductions is problematic in and of itself. The existence of deductions establishes the fact that taxation is inherently unjust and that those disparities must be

---

106   *Moatsos* (2021), 195.

corrected by allowing for deductions. The argument in favor of deductions is not convincing, since it would help everyone involved more if the rates themselves were decreased. It would also greatly reduce the time needed to calculate taxable income. In the Middle Ages, hierarchical society allowed for different tax rates depending on one's standing in the population because people were not seen as equal. Because people were seen as lesser than others, that warranted different taxes for different grades of humans. If one asks for equal rights, equal taxation is a must as well—but not in the various forms of socialism. This must apply to citizens and all forms of corporations.

Incorporating a flat tax is best done in conjunction with a great decrease in government spending. When using a flat tax, high-income earners would still generate the highest absolute revenue per person, even though the effective tax rates increase for low-income earners. Because everyone is taxed exactly relative to their income and there are no differing tax rates, there is no cold progression into higher brackets, regardless of inflation, and the equal rate does not deter people from earning higher incomes since they will always be taxed relative to their income. This is the only objectively correct implementation of an income tax without taking the dubious act of taxation itself into account. Taxation must become completely apolitical without incentivizing certain behaviors through deductions or different rates. In addition to the welfare state, progressive taxation is one of the most powerful instruments of oppression that social democrats can wield. Without it, people might still be taxed, but a flat tax distributes the burden of taxation equally, always relative to income. Only when percentages are equal can they tax incomes relative to their absolute values.

Tax allowances can only be taken seriously by those with an inner conflict, to the extent of *Goethe*'s Faust. One soul tells them that progressive taxation is just, while the other one proclaims that taxation is unjust—at least in regard to those earning lower incomes. They presuppose that a flat tax hurts low-income earners more than those who earn more money, which is mathematically impossible. Flat taxes are not regressive. If one imagines a regressive income tax, those people earning the most would have the lowest marginal and effective tax rates, while those in the lower brackets would be subject to the highest marginal and effective tax rates.

Flat taxes, on the other hand, are neither progressive nor regressive. Since the rate is flat and there exist no more deductions that could disadvantage some over others, the marginal tax rate is equal to the effective tax rate when the tax is flat. This is the most equitable proposal, since taxes levied in percentages are relative to whatever is being taxed. When one looks at absolute revenue from flat taxes, those who earn more pay more as well.

At a flat tax rate of 10 percent, someone earning $10,000 will pay $1,000 in income tax, while a person earning ten times as much pays exactly ten times the amount, even though both are subjected to the same relative rate of 10 percent. Unsurprisingly, those people alleging that flat taxes are regressive see flat corporate taxes as equitable and acceptable, since their hatred for corporations is systemic. While corporate taxes usually tend to tax profits, income taxes are levied on gross income. Because it makes little sense to tax corporate revenue since it would heavily discourage enterprising, one has to question the validity of taxing gross income from natural persons. Even though all forms of involuntary taxation skew the market, the goal should be to have as little market distortion as possible.

CORPORATE TAXATION AND FUTURE REVENUE

Some people complain that corporate tax rates have fallen globally in the last few decades. They do not seem to understand that the process of globalization is the main cause of this. Especially large companies, which indirectly shape the tax legislation in many countries, can no longer be forced to enterprise exclusively in their own country. If the tax rates are too high in a specific state, the companies will flee the country and decide to have their headquarters in a state with lower tax rates. To combat this legitimate and rational business strategy, many governments today are actively trying to establish a global minimum tax rate that would trap companies and subject them to a certain minimum rate, no matter where they operate. Fortunately, too many governments still profit from the attraction that lower taxes entail. As such, agreeing on a minimum tax rate is impossible if only a single prosperous state does not accept the agreement.

To make things worse for the social democracies around the world, companies will have greater leverage in the next few decades than ever before because they will no longer be as reliant on human employees, and neither individual people nor entire states are truly self-reliant. Higher corporate tax rates are not impossible, but quite unrealistic. This leaves social democratic states with no other option but to downsize. Restructuring entire states will be a time-consuming undertaking. Even so, it must be done. The decadence of social democratic governments has increased dramatically in the past few years. Many politicians and state employees are so distant from the market that they fail to understand the living conditions of the mean population, or what it takes to become wealthy. Although some politicians are jurists, most are economically inept, and in their uneducated financial illiteracy, they will increase debt further and spend more tax revenue every year, not understanding that the money is earned by real people, not just taxable persons. They are too obsessed with finding ways of turning all legislation into a piece of sociopolitical craftsmanship and apparently believe that subsidies generate wealth. In short, they live in a different reality, full of happy, helpless social democrats who look forward to paying taxes, welcome all legislation, and are generally well off, no matter the economic situation. The delta between reality and perceived political reality will increase further in the next few decades, providing the world with enough material to laugh about for at least the next few years. Because most forms of tax revenue will provide less revenue in the future, some ideas for supplementary taxes have been brought forward.

Nowadays, social democratic states are typically earning less revenue through taxes on goods and services[107]. This means they naturally increase their revenue elsewhere, especially in the areas of income tax, payroll tax, and contributions to social institutions. As the level of employment slowly decreases in the next few decades, the states will have to compensate by taxing goods and services more while slowly reducing the income tax and contributions to social institutions. Even while doing so, the state quota must necessarily decrease as the role of the government is reduced in importance in the twenty-first century. Governments that highly depend on income taxes and social security taxes will have to find other ways of raising revenue in the next few decades. Another, much easier option is to reduce government service, as this already eliminates

---

107   *OECD Tax on goods and services (indicator)* (2023).

large costs. The Hong Kong government has low single-digit debt, and its reliance on the income tax for revenue is fairly low as well. Contrasting this with any social democracy that levies both high income taxes and high social security taxes while having high debt immediately shows the gravity of this problem. In reality, the state will not considerably reduce its services or expenses voluntarily. In that case, new taxes must be levied.

Although a tax based on pure land value[108] has previously been suggested as a supplementary tax, incentivizing people to build on their property to reduce their tax burden, this does not take into account that a building boom would also expand dependence on debt even more. This could inevitably lead to a major economic housing bubble, especially when adopted by multiple governments. Although the alternative of permanently decreasing spending is not pleasing to the state sector, it is the only realistic solution if one wishes to preserve what little is left of the financial autonomy of coming generations.

Because the idea of central bank digital currencies has become much more popular in recent years, one alternative to the income tax, under a government without cash that only allows its digital currency as legal tender, is a transaction tax. Each transaction and act of using the currency could then include a 0.1 percent tax on top of the original transaction. Similar to the income

---

108   *Goodhart/Pradhan* (2020), 197.

tax, it would be an all-encompassing tax. The main difference is the lack of differentiation between a natural person and a legal person, so more economic activity could be redirected from tax planning to other, potentially more productive areas. The simple act of increasing marginal income tax rates is not a viable strategy and most likely does not increase government revenue beyond a certain threshold that is different for each population. It is also immediate that the gap between the brackets was wider in the past. In recent decades, the gap between median income and the threshold for the maximum marginal tax rate has decreased substantially. The result is that even though the marginal tax rates are lower, the tax base still grows substantially, allowing for more income tax revenue.

Additionally, the tax wedge is still unsustainably high[109], both of which further deter people from earning more money. As such, people who earn an income that is slightly higher than the median wage are typically subjected to a higher effective tax rate today than during times with marginal tax rates of over ninety percent. Since most states used to focus more on consumption taxes and state enterprises, the role of both might increase substantially in the next few decades to balance out the loss of revenue from individual taxes and social contributions. Even without taxation, governments still have numerous ways to finance their operations. Like

---

109   *OECD Tax wedge (indicator) (2023).*

any other business, they may directly price their products and services and allow people to buy them and subscribe to them. The myth that governments are only able to finance themselves through taxation is false. In the nineteenth century and pre-World War I twentieth century, Prussian state enterprises comprised over sixty percent of state revenue. The German railway alone amounted to almost fifty percent of state revenue, while direct and indirect taxes merely comprised single-digit percentages[110]. There exists no convincing argument to suggest that states are unable to repeat this in the future. Provided that they compete in the market, governments should become as big as they can if they can continue financing their expenses by selling goods and services to their citizens and beyond. Their healthcare, safety nets, pensions, and firefighters, among other examples, would have to compete with other insurers and service providers.

Although some people allege that certain services can fundamentally only be provided by the government, it is not evident why this is presumed to be the case. The only argument in favor of these state monopolies is the idea of an absolute state, who can choose whether to grant his subordinates access to the market or fully conquer positions for himself; this is quite in line with the social democratic dogma. On the other hand, many countries have voluntary firefighters who could easily

---

110   *Fremdling* (1980), 32.

turn their enthusiasm for firefighting into a job and compete with the government for customers, especially in more rural areas. They could sell their firefighting service in their effective radius as a subscription, including potential guarantees for extinguished fires. Alternatively, they can act as private firefighters and charge people based on the time they actually worked. The market would quickly decide whose firefighting services are the most reliable at the best price.

The same concept applies to any other service that people might have grown accustomed to as being unsuitable for the market. Although the state discourages natural monopolies from occurring in the market, it tends to think of its own monopolies as different since they are public, operate mostly without financial restraint of having to profit, while acting in the interest of the society[111]. Monopolies that are only able to be upheld through coercion are inherently objectionable. Those include monopoly state enterprises. However, if a government company competes in the market and succeeds in beating the competition while creating a monopoly for itself, the resulting monopoly is natural and unproblematic. Natural monopolies rarely occur, and when they do, the monopolist must compete even more thoroughly while continuing to please his customers—not an easy task. Out of the potential ideas for new revenue streams, the

---

111   *Maltsev (ed.)* (1993/2012), 8.

state enterprises seem the most compelling. They provide more sustainable revenue while reducing the overall burden on the population.

To curb the effects of decreasing tax revenue, introducing an upper limit on the number of state employees is necessary in an age of permanent low employment and a shift from the service sector economy to an entirely new sector that is soon to emerge from the onset of artificial general intelligence and superintelligence. Limiting the state sector to a percentage of employment is not convincing because, as the absolute number of employees falls in the next few decades, the relative number of persons employed in the state sector increases without any new persons needing to be employed. As such, it is more convincing to couple the allowed number of state sector employees to the number of citizens in the state. By choosing a sensible rate, such as a quarter of a percent to a percent, this forces them to become more productive or to reduce the tasks and duties of the state.

Both results are welcome. The alternate option is for all state employees to work without compensation. This would turn the state more into a form of charitable organization than a necessarily profitable one; therefore, it is even more unlikely to happen than the former idea of restructuring the state sector. Additionally, it is highly questionable whether enough people would seize the opportunity to truly serve the population, just like the high civil servants of the seventeenth and eighteenth centuries, who worked because they saw it as their honorable duty. Their roles as civil servants were also inheritable by their children. The system aimed to uphold state employment for only those persons honorable and selfless enough who could serve without regard for the necessity of gainful employment to uphold their standard of living. In later decades and centuries, this practice became increasingly uncommon until it fell out of practice completely. Today, everyone in the state sector is paid, even the high civil servants, such as ministers and heads of state. Especially politicians should not be compensated whatsoever. The idea that compensating politicians eliminates the need for lobbying and corruption is an alien idea; reality presents a different picture. When politicians are not compensated anymore, at least professional politicians will no longer be a threat.

RECAP

- Equal rights must also constitute equal taxation. Flat taxes, without the option to deduct anything, are the proper way of achieving this.
- The state must explore other ways of financing their expenses again.
- Taxes levied in percentages are the most equal because percentages are relative, not absolute.
- The differentiation between income tax and corporate tax is not convincing. If one realizes that higher corporate taxes are not feasible and severely inhibit the ability of companies to enterprise, the same applies to natural persons.
- Government revenue, in the form of individual taxes and social contributions, will decrease in the future. Those states that are not overly reliant on the aforementioned income streams will fiscally outperform those that are.
- When properly implemented, state enterprises can reduce the economic burden the state has on the population.

7. ECONOMICS VERSUS SOCIALISM

SUBJECTIVISM AND THE MARKET

The most important concept in economics is subjectivism. It suggests that people inherently see goods as goods because of their own subjective views on the quality of said good[112]. Objectivity, on the other hand, does not exist in economics, as no one could ever grasp the many subjective opinions of other people interacting with each other in the economy. The economy itself comprises the entirety of interactions between market participants. As such, human action is equivalent to the economy. The market, on the other hand, is merely a subdivision of the economy but not necessarily part of a local economy. It does not have to be a physical place to facilitate interactions between the market participants. Because markets are a theoretical concept and not physical, market failure is logically impossible. Since markets are parts of the economy, which comprises human action, one would have to deny human action and accuse all market participants of not acting in their own interests to perceive anything near a market failure. There is no such thing as a market goal; only individual

---

112   *Harper/Endres* (2022), 222.

goals comprise the market in its totality. Some rulers do dislike that individuals may stray from their supposedly enlightened goals, but that does not constitute the existence of market failures. More so, it illustrates that they have failed themselves in perpetuating their opinion of what should constitute an economy or a successful market. An example is the concept of a planned economy, which is goal-driven and regulated. Even when personifying them, because markets are not inherently goal-driven, the populist phrase of market failure is a theoretical and practical impossibility and cannot apply to the free market.

The participants in the market always come up with an optimal solution, but by no means the best for special interest groups. Unfree markets, plagued by government intervention, promise just that, which is why they are so popular with special interest groups, regardless of status and level of wealth. The free market, in contrast to the unfree market, is therefore a system of compromises that leads to wealth and prosperity instead of stagnation and poverty. The only markets that can fail are those that are being controlled and intervened by governments, thereby skewing natural decision-making and human action. The concept of market failure is supposed to empower further intervention leading to an intervention spiral, induce a false sense of superiority in economic planners, install a permanent fear of market failure in the population, and divert attention away from the regulation responsible for the perceived failure.

PLANNED ECONOMIES

The concept of a free market, devoid of intervention, completely contrasts with the ideologies that proponents of planned economies and regulation have. Economic planners base their inherent view of the economy on a form of utilitarianism in which the perceived greater good of the collective trumps the free market and the individual acting in it. The process of intervening on behalf of special interest groups is enough to warrant restrictions in the market economy. Thinking one can outperform the free market using a method of compromise between different special interest groups is one of the biggest economic fallacies that social democrats pursue regularly. All special interest groups with worthwhile ideas or positions in the market already have enough bargaining power. Those who do not succeed in the free market often feel that it is inherently unfair. They feel the need to fix the market; to make it more inclusive and equal. They fail to recognize, however, that the free market is impossible for any human to fully grasp and that intervening creates more problems in the long term than it could ever subjectively correct.

For those economic planners and regulators, the meaning of individual opinion recedes into obscurity. They substitute it with the collective opinion, and typically they will quote the greater good as well—an unquantifiable measurement that is supposed to guide and nudge legislators in the correct direction. It is supposed to balance the economy, as if it were a game, by evaluating the weaknesses of an economic actor and legislating accordingly. To protect the alleged infantile and helpless consumer, the massive amount of consumer protection legislation helps nudge the market in favor of the consumer. This seems like a great idea to many semi-educated people who only mean well. After all, the weak consumer is seen as so oblivious to his own actions that not having carefully established policies in place must appear like a grave endangerment of the consumer, who would frankly be completely helpless without them. It is their belief that the company and the entrepreneur are inherent oppressors. The fact that any enterprising individual needs customers to sell goods or services to, is completely ignored in the policymaking bubble. In turn, a few subjective economic opinions control how many people live their lives today.

While it is impossible to always assume malicious intent, it is legitimate to think that many legislators are led by a futile vision of a better human, only achievable through change from above. The collective trumps every individual and is protected by the enlightened policies of the well-meaning legislator. In the socialist view, the individual can only experience true freedom when it is part of the collective. But, even if a planner had a new snapshot of the whole economy every second, he would not be able to allocate resources and calculate prices more effectively than in the free market. Quick responses to changes in a planned economy are impossible. This is upsetting to some of those who have exceptionally high intelligence in certain areas, consider themselves intellectuals, or went to prestigious schools. They want planned and scientific solutions to the irrational problems of the market. To make things worse, planned economies cause disastrous outcomes for nature and the environment[113] because they either try to secure as much employment as possible, at any cost, or exploit resources beyond necessary levels to work towards their goal-oriented economy. In the process, they contaminate their living spaces, resulting in polluted and uninhabitable areas[114]. Such results can be seen in the former Soviet Union and even observed in modern communist China. Nature is much better off in countries where free market interactions occur more frequently between market participants. The planners believe innovation is created through forced, enlightened policy and regulation, even though there is no motivation to succeed or be more efficient if one cannot act freely or gets subsidized and punished at the will of politicians.

MARGINALISM

Contrary to the objectivity of the economic planner, marginalism is an economic principle based on the fact

---

113   *Osoba* (1996), 176.
114   *Henry/Douhovnikoff* (2008), 438.

that resources are scarce in this world. It assumes that all goods and services have a subjective utility associated with them. The theory assumes that goods are anything we recognize as being able to satisfy our desires. As human desires are subjective, one desire does not appear as such to another person. The higher the quantity of a good or service and the more frequently it is produced, consumed, or hoarded, the more its marginal utility diminishes. Someone who is hungry will value the utility of food more than someone who just finished eating a multi-course meal. For that reason, gold is worth more to most people than water. This, however, is contrasted when one finds himself in a precarious situation that inverses the utility of water and gold[115]. Adam Smith understood that as the standard of living increases, the demand for goods increases as well[116]. This is why, historically, economic growth coincided with considerable increases in the standard of living.

Economic growth and inequality

Economic growth is one of the most important economic indicators for any given nation. To illustrate this, one can use a cake. If one standard-sized cake is to be distributed between thirty people instead of three, the chance of fully feeding everyone is close to zero. If the

---

115 *Menger* (1871/2022), 135.
116 *Smith/Cannan (ed.)* (1776/1903), 71.

cake grows in size and mass, however, more people will have the chance to be fed. This is why theories of economic degrowth tread dangerous waters. Similar to the cake example, when a population stagnates or is reduced considerably while the wealth stagnates but does not decrease, those people still alive will have a chance to become wealthier than before. This explains why the demographic change does not have to be a purely negative event. Although the demographic change does coincide with an economic period of uncertainty, the hypothetical income inequality of artificial superintelligence taking over most sectors of the economy does prove to be a more considerable risk, which may lead to unrest in the population.

Those income inequalities can therefore only be solved with more economic growth, not more redistribution; it is overt that an act of redistribution does not create wealth. People who allege it stimulates the economy forget that redirecting the economic activity of wealthier people to less wealthy people does not create more wealth. The total wealth of the nation would not increase since the wealthier person would have originally spent his money at a different enterprise or saved it to further invest it afterwards. Just because one company would not exist without access to redistributed wealth in the form of welfare money being spent at the company does not lead to a decrease in total wealth since the market is not a zero-sum game.

If one truly believes that redistribution stimulates the individuals in the market, then one should have no problem with a fixed universal basic income that allows everyone to spend some money but still be unable to retain wealth. Evaluating this situation using the small cake that is supposed to feed thirty people, as described above, one would end up with a situation where everyone has a small piece of the cake while never being fully fed and unable to receive a full piece of the cake. To allow people to be entitled to their share of the cake, depending on their status in the market, seems much more reasonable and morally sound—albeit not conducive to further equality, which has no place in the market anyway, unless one wishes for widespread impoverishment, which is the only effective way of equalizing, using rule from above.

Although the data on income inequality is indifferent, the argument in favor of it makes clear that income inequality has increased in the past few decades, at least in many First World countries, since economic growth has not occurred on a large enough scale while the welfare state continues to redistribute, especially the wealth of middle- and lower-class people. This does not mean that wealthier people are too wealthy. It simply appears that the middle class and lower class were forced into a position of guaranteed economic uncertainty by being the primary groups that participate in and finance the welfare state. State welfare reduces individual wealth while creating a new system of often abstract claims against specific state institutions. Redistribution therefore hurts wealth accumulation and is inherently unable to decrease inequality by empowering economic actors. It does, however, increase it whenever it strains the wealthier people or those who would become wealthier without the artificial limitation on their wealth. By slowly ruining the chances of the middle class in a country, one can guarantee the relative primacy of the truly wealthy people in any given population.

The ideology of stakeholder capitalism advocates a similar world structure in which the broad population is incapable of fully participating in the market, while few societal stakeholders can assume a higher percentage of the broad wealth. This is achievable by introducing a universal basic income that is high enough to live on but low enough for the average person to be continuously bound to the state. Some social democratic elitists imagine a technocratic socialist utopia and are ready to do everything in their power to ensure that it becomes a reality. In a real market economy everyone is a stakeholder automatically because each individual benefits from the other's success in the form of higher standards of living and wealth that they would not have previously obtained if not for the free market. In that case, the term stakeholder loses its meaning. As the stakeholders of stakeholder capitalism can be freely defined, however, the members of various large NGOs[117]show great interest in operating in favor such idea, and not against it. Their livelihood depends on the prolonged success of social democracies. To achieve this, the elitist-acting members of various NGOs, foundations, governments, and corporations closely work together with one another. The multinational corporations provide numerous jobs for the population, which generates tax revenue, and in exchange, they are allowed to keep most of their wealth since they have access to immaculate tax planning. All popular political orientations have been undermined by misinformation nowadays, to establish social democracy as the allegedly only viable system in the twenty-first century. No matter who or what people vote for in a social democracy, the masses may vote but never decide; the role of the citizen and the state must always stay the same. Democratism is propagated not because it is good but because those involved with high stakes are afraid that a change of system would halt the global economy. This problem is further amplified by some day-to-day operations being completely dependent on the state monopolies, or at least relative stability, such as running water, plumbing, or electricity. Even if that means upholding social democracy.

---

117   Footnote 1, loc. cit.

DIVISION OF LABOR

The division of labor is a natural and decentralized process that causes people to divide labor among those who specialize in different parts of the supply chain. The process of globalization after World War II has certainly helped the division of labor. Isolationism, on the other hand, limits the potential division of labor to disguise a lack of competitiveness. Truly free civilizations can only benefit from globalization in the long run. Some special interest groups definitely do not benefit from globalization and the division of labor, and as a result, isolationism is still seen as a viable option for many people. That being said, customs, duties, and taxes prevent true free trade from occurring on a large scale, even today in a world of far fewer tarrifs than even one hundred years ago. The isolationist policy is sustainable, but it does limit wealth in the long term. Especially in a world where everyone is dependent, to a certain degree, on goods and services from other countries, isolationism should not be pursued.

OPPORTUNITY COST AND TIME PREFERENCE

The cost of a good or service is the opportunity cost compared to a different one. If a person has the choice between buying something and forgoing the purchase, he will have to evaluate whether the opportunity cost of buying the item outweighs the cost of forgoing the purchase. The preference to forgo or buy is strongly affected by planned and regulated economies. In addition to forgoing certain purchases or choosing between different goods, time preference makes some people savers and others spenders. High time preference manifests in high present consumption and spending, while someone with low time preference values future consumption and spending over the present. Countless factors determine time preference. The broad population today gravitates towards a high time preference due to the deliberate distortion of markets and the fact that many people have access to government safety nets, which reduces the necessity of saving and investing. At least if one believes that state welfare is sustainable in its current form. Another factor that increases time preference is the inflation of the money supply.

Although the term has been overused, in reality, inflation is only a term used when describing how the money supply inflates. The inflation is commonly measured using the consumer price index, which has historically been changed multiple times in its methodology to lower reported inflation. It should not be trusted since it assumes that the consumer substitutes goods and services whenever they become too expensive. It is also dynamic, not fixed, meaning that the figurative basket of goods and services changes frequently. Money is a good like any other, and as such, it diminishes in value and marginal utility whenever there is more of it in circulation. Because of inflation, price increases occur, although price increases are not synonymous with inflation and vice versa. If the increase in the money supply (in percent) is greater than the current interest rate, savers and investors do not generate enough interest while the money they still have devalues. This will eventually lead to a higher time preference and spending increases because people become afraid of their currency losing its value in the future. As such, they would rather spend it in the present if the opportunity cost of spending outweighs not spending the currency at all.

INTEREST RATES

Interest rates can be used to measure the time preference of the broad population. At least in a free market where banks can set their own interest rates. In restricted economies today, interest rates are set by central banks around the world according to monetary goals that benefit special interest groups. This is one characteristic of planned economies. If interest rates are low, many people are bound to spend more and get into debt more frequently. Governments and companies get used to cheap money, and over the long term, they overleverage or become dependent on debt to finance their operations. When interest rates rise to levels higher than the rate of inflation, people save more because they can generate more money in the future if they refrain from spending it all in the present.

Companies are also less likely to overleverage in a high-interest environment since interest payments on their loans are much higher. Interest is important because it gives people an incentive to save money, which creates wealth. If no one had ever saved money to invest it, civilizations could not have become wealthier.

Prices and Price Controls

In a market economy, prices change constantly, according to the people willing to buy or sell[118]. This occurs because nothing has any intrinsic or objective value except what people see it as and are willing to buy and sell it for. Prices must therefore always be subjective. When person A tries selling a self-made chair for $600, but the only buyer is person B, who is willing to pay $300, the subjective value of the chair to person A, who built it, does not correspond with the opinion of B, as expressed by the $300 that he is willing to pay. Even if it cost person A $500 to source the materials and build the chair, this does not have to necessarily influence the price. Although A might be hesitant to sell the chair at a loss, this risk is inherent in any market interaction. Profit is not guaranteed in a market. When transacting, prices are a way to measure cost, calculate, and allocate scarce resources by noting how people respond to the given prices. They are inherently subjective, which is why one person might pay more

---

118   *Cantillon/Murphy (ed.)* (1734/2015), 56.

money for a good or a service than another person, simply because the opportunity costs differ. In social democracies, price controls have mostly gone out of fashion, although in times of crisis, they are reimplemented sometimes. Wage controls, however, have become an irrevocable component of social democratism. The so-called minimum wage is an arbitrary wage calculated by politicians, legislators, and lobbyists that prevents those without proper qualifications from being employed in the competitive labor market.

The only two people who should be involved in setting a wage are the employer and the employee. After all, employment is a trade like any other. It is a trade that offers forgoing time and labor in exchange for monetary compensation. In other words, a voluntary transaction between market participants. The goal of a transaction is for all participants to benefit from it more than if they had not transacted in the first place. In a market economy, one has the choice of how, whether, or with whom one wants to transact. In social democracies, this autonomy is always reduced through legislation, meaning that some economic actors can be forced to or prevented from transacting at will. When a transaction is forced or completed using an act or threat of violence, it loses its inherent properties of being a transaction. Similarly, high minimum wages that do not correlate with the economic performance that warrants such a wage will cause companies to perform much worse. The higher the wages become, the less competitive a company becomes, which reduces employment opportunities for at least those people in low-paying positions. The alternative to paying lower wages is that products and services either become more expensive, the quality degrades over time, or the company becomes less profitable, all of which are undesirable because they make the company less competitive. Minimum wage legislation therefore corrupts the market noticably.

COMPETITION

Because all economic actors compete with each other, at least indirectly, the market does not allow success to occur forever. Without failure, there would be no competition and no new success. Both success and failure are the catalysators of innovation and change. State subsidies, bailouts, and legislation preventing competition from occurring, all disrupt the economy. Companies and individuals who should fail are prevented from doing so, while others are prevented from succeeding. The majority of people, two centuries ago, worked as farmers. If governments had subsidized these farmers constantly and prevented technology, machines, and innovation from entering that field, most people today would still be farmers. The standard of living would suffer as a result. Old things must often perish to let new things flourish. Those people unqualified for new kinds of employment who had their employment terminated because of a harsh shift in technology will often fight new technology and hold a grudge against those who replaced them. Later generations may reap the benefits of the previous unemployment; they won't, however, care about the loss of employment for a distant previous generation. It is therefore problematic that uneducated people believe the market is a zero-sum game. They think that when one person is successful, another must lose—often seeing themselves in the position of the loser. This is obvious nonsense and must be combated with proper education. It appears that in most countries, people with lower education have a more negative attitude towards the term capitalism[119]. This means that education must play a larger role in the future, unless the goal is to make the mean population more susceptible to populism, in which case economic education must be fully eliminated.

EMPLOYMENT

Many social democrats believe that high employment is necessary for a productive population and a functional economy. As people became more productive in the past, they started to work fewer hours, let machines do their work, or found more efficient solutions to problems. In a free market of interactions, every time something becomes more productive, someone or something less productive will stop being used. Because

---

119 *Zitelmann* (2022), 346.

this is a natural process, at some point in time, humans will naturally stop working because productive employment will no longer exist for humans. No company would then be left that would benefit from their productivity. We are far from that standard, though, and using UBI at the expense of a few extremely productive people causes people to become less productive overall because they are living at the expense of others instead of becoming productive enough to not have any need for employment as a means to retain their lifestyle and standard of living. Proponents of redistributive mechanisms, such as UBI, need to use future tax income and government debt as collateral to finance their system.

Parkinson's Law describes that work expands to fill the available time. This is especially relevant when evaluating the role and size of the state sector, which is typically not subject to the principles of market competition. *Parkinson* elaborates that, through real or imaginary feelings of overwork, government employees appoint subordinates to assist them. To make things worse, the more employees and the more steps to completion exist, the more the work multiplies. The official has to correct the mistakes of the subordinates, does not end up being less overworked, and the same amount of work has been handled and processed by more people than before. In the end, even though they are all busy, the amount of work done has not increased[120]. One would be led to believe that in the age of technology, government employees should become more efficient, work less, and employ fewer people. Reality shows that this does not occur in the state sector because there exists no incentive to operate a profitable state agency or office. In addition to low profitability, the more bloated governments are, the more their productivity actually decreases[121].

Social democratic governments are therefore unable to become more productive as time passes without also decreasing the number of institutions and programs they uphold. Because government spending rates do not decrease over time in social democracies, it is entirely unlikely that the productivity of social democratic governments will increase beyond a certain threshold unless they incorporate artificial intelligence into their operations and reduce the number of human employees accordingly.

Even then, humans will be the ones to slow down the operation, and productivity will decrease over time. As a matter of fact, in the non-state sector, labor productivity is stagnant in most First World countries. It is even declining in some countries[122]. It appears that most First World countries are unable to become more productive

---

120   *Parkinson* (1958), 10.
121   *Schuknecht/Tanzi/Afonso* (2003), 24.
122   *OECD Labour productivity forecast (indicator)* (2023).

without more sophisticated technology. The poorer countries, on the other hand, will still experience a rise in productivity for some time since they are not as productive yet.

Accountability

The free market is built on trust. When legislation and lobbying allow untrustworthy market participants, the whole concept of a free market is not possible anymore. This is because everyone needs to be accountable. The market cannot function without accountability. No economic actor, no matter his position, should be exempt from accountability in the market. Claims against other people must be enforced by some means. If this is not done, property is left unprotected, since anyone could engage in fraud or theft without being punished. Although debatable, history does suggest that in large organizational structures, such as the state, these claims can be enforced more effectively than by individual actors acting on behalf of themselves. Especially in a world where people can easily flee countries and fly across continents in mere hours.

Neoliberalism as Socialdemocratic Neologism

Since it has now been established that social democracies actively act contrary to liberal values, including the market economy, it is quite troublesome that the current economic system is often described as neoliberalism. This cannot be more than a deliberate attempt at slandering liberalism, since this socialism has little to do with its opposing system of liberalism. Similarly, the term social market economy, used primarily in Europe, has been misappropriated by social democrats for their own purposes. Originally, the economist *Ludwig Erhard* proposed that the market economy was a social system because of its inherent nature[123] of allowing people to amass wealth and escape poverty, thereby calling it the social market economy. He saw any kind of attempt of subordinating the market to social requisites as heresy[124].

Even so, the social democratic movement considered this term to be an open invitation to regulate and try to combine socialism with the market economy. This then led to abominable neologisms, such as socialized or humane market economy. Another term, as explained previously, is stakeholder capitalism, which is used more frequently nowadays in North America. This term is just as twisted, since it presupposes that there exist fixed inherent stakeholders in the market. It can be assumed that those who propagate this system do believe that they are in such a position, similar to an oligarchy.

---

123   *von Hayek/Bartley III (ed.)* (1988), 117.
124   *Wünsche* (2015), 30.

Recap

- In the market everything is subjective. This includes prices and marginal utility. Objectivity does not exist.
- Since resources are scarce, people compete with each other.
- Markets cannot fail because they are not goal-driven.
- Redistribution is unable to create wealth. Wealth is created through economic growth.
- Every economic actor must be held accountable.
- Time preference is affected by internal and external factors.
- Preventing unemployment through subsidies, legislation, and bailouts corrupts the core of the market economy.
- Profit is never guaranteed in a market economy.

8. Debt and spending

Debt and deficits

When evaluating the increase in debt in different nations, one cannot merely look at the state debt, since high household debt can also be an indicator of an increased risk of insolvency. High corporate debt can be an indicator of extreme reliance on debt. Those companies are commonly known as zombie companies because they can only stay afloat by going into debt. It appears that some countries are disproportionately affected by this phenomenon[125]. The countries in the dataset in which the debt of non-financial corporations comprises more than 100 percent of the GDP are Belgium, Canada, China, Denmark, Finland, France, Hong Kong, Ireland, Japan, Korea, Luxembourg, the Netherlands, Singapore, Sweden, and Switzerland. Although none of the other countries have a non-financial corporate sector with acceptable levels of debt, only four of the evaluated countries have a household and NPISH debt level of over 100 percent of GDP: Australia, Canada, Korea, and Switzerland. The latter

---

125　Own calculations. *Bank of International Settlements* (2023); *International Monetary Fund* (2023).

three out of the four also have a non-financial corporate sector with debt levels higher than 100 percent of GDP. The government levels of debt are widely known to be unsustainable in many states and shall not be reiterated here. But high debt is not the only danger. In addition to high debt, except for the year 2000, the United States government has maintained a deficit since the data was collected in 1970. Norway, on the other hand, has had no deficit since at least 1995, with the exception of 2020[126]. When the time comes to transition social democracies into a new system, those states with high debt and deficits will face harsh realities.

Deficits must be punished and explicitly outlawed in constitutions, since by going into a deficit the state directly influences the future capital allocation of its citizens. The citizens have to pay to compensate for the deficits with higher taxes or future austerity measures. State deficits do increase the implicit state debt considerably when they become the norm. To rule out further hidden increases in implicit debt, the state needs to start using double-entry bookkeeping. The cameralism of the seventeenth century and beyond must be overcome. Cameralist accounting, although favored by state employees, is intransparent and results in anyone using it appearing untrustworthy because it propagates single-entry bookkeeping. Because of its intransparency and lack of focus on profitability,

---

126   *OECD General government deficit (indicator)* (2023).

cameralism is a state favorite. The thin line between encouraging high debt and high inflation can lead to short-term economic miracles but also high volatility. This results in economic bubbles and subsequent harsh economic corrections that call for the same state measures that intervene in the market and led to the economic distortions in the first place. The longer this process continues, the more the market must be distorted, and discontinuing such practices is almost impossible without compromising the temporal well-being of millions of people who are used to living in such a debt-financed world—entirely without savings. An example of a harsh economic correction is the economic boom in Japan in the 1980s, caused by high debt and an increasing money supply. This situation was then worsened by the shift towards a service economy, which caused another building boom fueled by low-interest money lending[127].

Georg Friedrich Knapp, arguably the founder of chartalism, lived in the same intellectual age as cameralism. Chartalism inspired Keynesianism and Modern Monetary Theory and therefore has an important place in social democratic policies. Cameralism and chartalism do still dominate, at least in the minds of many people who are responsible for envisioning legislation and policies. In that world view, the state must be the primate; everything must be

---

127   *Quinn/Turner* (2020), 138f.

subordinate to the state. Only in this world view can tax avoidance become theft, since the state must also logically be entitled to whatever it is entitled to. The advocates of cameralism have worked hard to ensure that the prevailing opinion today alleges that private accounting must not be compared to state accounting. Doing so would unquestionably show the accounting fraud involved. The fanatical theory of cameralism is so engrained in the state that many modern theories that assign the state a large role in world affairs are based on cameralism. This includes social democatism to some extent. The evolution of chartalism, called modern monetary theory, even proposes a job guarantee for everyone[128]. This completely debases the market and all its economic actors. It also completely rejects the notion of the natural rate of unemployment[129], which cannot be reduced further by state spending.

Keynes' influence

Keynesians, chartalists, and advocates of modern monetary theory all fall for the fallacy that only the act of spending money results in wealth. However, this is debunked if one imagines a situation in which one dollar is in circulation. Person A receives the dollar and spends it. Person B, who is on the receiving end, now has one dollar but spends it again, since spending must result in

---

128 *Drumetz/Pfister* (2021), 358.
129 *Makin/Tunny* (2021), 4.

wealth according to Keynesiansism. This results in person B spending the dollar and person C receiving it. Persons A, B, and C can now repeat this process indefinitely but will never become wealthy. Only once one person realizes he has to save at least one part of the dollar to retain any kind of wealth he can use to invest will wealth be created. Only saving money and investing the savings in capital to generate even more money in return can lead to wealth. The Keynesians, chartalists, and modern monetary theorists allege that their economic theory is only applicable on a large scale, not between individual economic actors. Unfortunately, these economic theories do not function without their mathematical models, which create synthetic models, data, and numbers while proclaiming to be theories built on empirical evidence.

The socialist economist *Piketty,* in his flawed book on capital in the twenty-first century, manipulates and fakes data on wealth and rising inequality[130]. He also severely overestimates the role of multigenerational wealth while underestimating the reactions to potential wealth taxes that his colleagues and he himself have proposed for years. In his eyes, there are only wealthy capital owners who accumulate wealth at the expense of everyone else. At the very least, *Piketty* understands the fallacy of purely mathematical models that some economists fabricate. The productivity of capital has

---

130   *Delsol (ed.)/Lecaussin (ed.)/Martin (ed.) et al.* (2017), 94, 135.

increased over the decades. This is positive because it means that less capital is needed today to achieve the same growth as in previous decades and centuries. To illustrate this concept with an example, one can look at computers. Modern twenty-first century personal computers are cheaper, smaller, and more effective than the large enterprise servers of the 1950s. This does not mean enterprise-level computing solutions are limited to personal computers, though. The modern server is obviously more productive and expensive than the personal computer. Because capital is more productive compared to the twentieth century, the role of non-human and personal wealth has increased in importance[131].

Social democracies, however, fundamentally oppose the accumulation of wealth, as seen in the efforts to redistribute and tax alleged excess wealth. The old social democratic paradigm of the welfare state being the wealth of the worker does not stand in the twenty-first century. In European countries and North America, median wealth increased onefold to threefold, on average, in the last two decades alone[132]. Trying to focus primarily on state provision therefore seems to be a mistake, being unable to offset the importance of wealth in the mean population. The aforementioned economic schools of thought believe that the state monopoly of currency must be exploited to the maximum by inflating

---

131   *Davies/Lluberas/Shorrocks* (2017), 757.
132   *UBS/Credit Suisse* (2023), 26.

the economy and creating unsustainable employment, which must fail once the money stops flowing or the economy is corrected. To remove this risk entirely, they advocate an economy built on debt and inflation, thereby hurting the saver[133] the most. Although *Keynes* tries to hide his contempt for the rentier, his love for regulating the value of the currency stems from a fundamental hatred of the alleged rentier class. Although he did acknowledge that post-World War I inflation had wiped out the savings of the middle class, he does also suggest «[that] each generation can disinherit in part its predecessors' heirs» by inflating the money supply and reducing the value of money[134].

He also suggests «[...] the reason why the leadership of the capitalist cause is weak and stupid» is the alleged hereditary principle of the system[135]. Again, he sees the rare intergenerational rentier as the norm. He feels an urge to remove this perceived inequality from the earth —not by brute measures but through monetary policy. He understood the importance of inflation and the effects it can have on the whole population. His views on policy were strange to begin with. In eugenic fashion, Keynes, who believed in reforming nations through policy, thought that the large population of Russia was detrimental to the economic future of the country. He advised the state to establish a balanced budget for

---

133   *Keynes* (1931/2010), 75.
134   *Keynes* (1931/2010), 64, 67.
135   *Keynes* (1931/2010), 299.

population[136]. Such an idea seems even more morbid when one realizes the tens of millions that died under the Soviet communists alone.

Keynes, who is related to socialist thought through the Fabian Society[137], Eugenics Society, and the British Labour Party, thereby comes to false conclusions about the rentier, seeing him as a homogenous class that must be shunned. He forgets that the rentier, although not engaged in manual labor, is unable to increase his wealth himself if he does not provide his capital to others or uses his capital to provide services to others. If he hoards his money without investing it, he will not have much of it in the long term. He is therefore an integral part of any population. Even the rare intergenerational rentier serves a great purpose. He can provide services more sustainably than the person who has to use debt first to accumulate capital. People who believe in the paradox of thrift allege that everyone else who does not is not thinking beyond the individual household or talking about a barter economy and obviously is unable to see the full, enlightened, monetarist picture.

In reality, these people are the ones who do not understand the difference between saving and hoarding. *Keynes* misunderstanding of saving is the reason for his hatred of the rentier. In his mind, saving was an act of

---

136   *Toye* (1997), 14.
137   *Fuller* (2019), 145.

inaction. He did not fully grasp these mistakes, but at least he knew that excess inflation does not just cause more destruction but also more injustice among the population. In the classical sense, hoarding reduces saving[138]. Hoarded money is unproductive, while saved money is productive in an economy because it needs to be spent on investments to remain productive. Similar to savings, capital that is not productive is not capital. The claim that hoarding reduces economic activity is true, but it has nothing to do with saving money. Similarly, MMT proponents believe that savings are net government debt holdings. As such, using their false definition of saving, the theory suggests that the private sector could never save without the state sector incurring debt. Saving actually grows the economy, and most people could greatly benefit from saving more of their money. Even paying back debt is a form of saving because the reoccurring payments fall away at some point. Many modern Keynesians choose to ignore the overwhelming evidence against the alleged paradox because it does ruin large parts of the Keynesian theory, namely the focus on constant spending.

Although it is sometimes attributed to *Keynes* that he was a secret communist who tried to establish communist reign by inflating away the savings of the people, in reality, this theory holds little merit[139], and he most likely was just misinformed. The reason why some

---

138   *Ahiakpor* (1995), 17, 19, 28f.
139   *Hazlitt* (1965), 468f.

people allege that *Keynes* was a communist is that his ties to the socialist Fabian Society are certainly controversial. Especially the well-known members *Sydney Webb, Beatrice Webb,* and *George Bernard Shaw* were proponents of various socialist states, including the national socialist and communist states. Because *John Maynard Keynes* also advocated a monetary policy of intervention, especially inflation, some people like to conclude that the baron must have been a secret communist. In reality, he was most likely a moderate socialist—in other words, a social democrat. *Keynes* did praise the Soviet Union, but he never saw the same radical change as being possible in Great Britain. Today, one can only speculate if this is because of his eugenic inclinations—he perceived the British to be superior to the Soviets—or because he knew that such radical change would be desasterous even to his own imaginative plans. The fact is, although *Keynes* did show tendencies to fully support the communist system, he could never truly embrace it. Together with the secret Soviet spy *Harry Dexter White,* he was also involved in propaganda for the Soviet Union.

Bretton Woods system

Both played the most important roles in establishing the Bretton Woods system. Both men certainly did not see communism as a threat and were apologetic, or at least indifferent, to it. The Bretton Woods member countries agreed to establish the World Bank, the International Monetary Fund, and the Bank for Reconstruction and Development. The system stopped the competitive devaluation of currencies by pegging the value of said currencies to the US dollar. Only a marginal deviation from the pegged value was allowed. The dollar itself was pegged to gold at a fixed rate of 35 dollars for one ounce of gold. This meant that anyone could exchange 35 dollars for one ounce of gold. As such, the US dollar became the reserve currency for many of the world's most economically important countries. As the United States emitted more currency in the late 1960s and early 1970s, starting in 1971, the US dollar was unpegged from gold. Soon afterwards, the Bretton Woods system collapsed. Only the aforementioned organizations still exist today. Although the governments still intervene with monetary policy, the formerly pegged currencies are allowed to deviate enough to create floating exchange rates.

Although the gold standard and a deflationary environment are objectively better than inflation, the prerequesites are investments to fall back on once employment is terminated due to economic corrections. As such, it is currently not possible to have long-term deflation because it would impoverish the broad population without savings. When the broad population reduces its consumption and invests more money instead, deflation must follow to retain the wealth. In an inflationary environment without employment opportunities for the masses, the companies that are able to profit from the increased non-human productivity in the twenty-first century would go against the interests of the investing population, who live off their investments and therefore must dislike inflation. For politicians, it is increasingly difficult to manage an inflationary environment that objectively penalizes savers of the past, with possible deflationary periods that disadvantage those financial illiterates who have nothing but their employment as their income. In the past, the inflationary environment has won, leading to the expropriation of investors.

It will be interesting to see whether this continues in the next few decades. If this is the case, one must earn as much money as humanly possible to accumulate investments before mass unemployment becomes the new norm. It appears that the best way to protect the interests of both parties is to have neither inflation nor deflation—not a synthesis of both. Having a fixed value for a currency is much more desirable than trying to balance inflation and deflation and pandering to one specific group at a time. Since economics is frequently perverted by politicians, constitutionally setting a fixed value of a currency would be a necessary step in the right direction if the state monopoly of currency were to be preserved. If not, many different currencies with different economic properties can be thought of and realized, as an alternative to the currency monopoly.

BANKING

Centralized currencies also need centralized banks to succeed long-term. If the regulation of banks is different within the structure and the collateral and equity are not the same, then the entire financial system becomes unstable. Financial banking models that hide volatility must be prevented. Full reserve banking, preventing banks from creating money through lending, and limiting accessibility to debt are the most important ways to create long-term stability in the banking sector. Certainly, in the short term, this would result in large economic corrections, but both the financial and non-financial sectors have too much debt to be sustainable in the long term. The short-term thinking, especially in the financial sector, created an environment where even households gladly took on debt simply to live in a depreciating asset—their own house. Fractional reserve banking has caused much harm to the world economy, especially by setting the groundwork for the intense economic distortions that must lead to corrections, such as the Great Depression, the recent Financial Collapse of 2008, or the COVID-19 Crash of 2020. It would be naive to ignore the threat of the banking system's ability to create currency ex nihilo, through debt.

When people deposit their cash with their bank of choice, the cash turns into a claim against the bank in form of checkbook money, amounting to the original cash deposit. The actual cash is not stored in some fictional individual customer vault. Instead, the cash is used either as a minimal bank reserve, to service the claims of other bank customers, or to be paid out through small loans. When the person who originally deposited the cash wants to get back that exact currency, it is unable to receive the original currency because the currency is no longer in the property of the bank. The customer can invoke his claim against the bank. If he is lucky, his debtor, the bank, will have enough cash available to service his claim. If not, and others realize this, a multitude of people might desperately try to have their claims serviced, and the resulting bank run can lead to the affected bank having to register for insolvency.

The innertia of the bank run can spill over to other financial institutions and cause a financial crisis. All banks that operate on a fractional reserve basis must constantly work in fear of shutting down their enterprise. To compensate for the risky banking operation, the banking sector leverages a lot. Although risk management rules are put into place to combat speculative operations, the financial sector is hard-wired to think short-term and will find its way around the legislation. Since legislation has given banks the privilege of creating currency *ex nihilo*, it is only fitting if those privileges are taken away. This is certainly more effective than trying to box in the financial sector and then regulating the result. The legislation is responsible for allowing the fractional reserve banking system. As such, all calls for more regulation are inappropriate, since the underlying cause of the volatility are the privileges that cause the bank to only be able to work in speculative and risky ways. Natural persons are unable to create money by lending, so it only makes sense that banks be subjected to the same logic. If one does not have money, he cannot lend it to someone else. Because the banks create money simply by giving out loans, the risk of not paying back the loan on time lies completely with the debtor since the creditor is mostly not using his own money.

Although currency emitted by states does not have to hold inherent value, the stability of the currency is arguably even more important than the underlying value of the currency itself. If a currency depreciates or appreciates at a constant rate every year, the result either hurts creditors or debtors. Currencies that wildly fluctuate between appreciating and depreciating every year hurt both because no one can calculate properly in those economic conditions. The state, typically the largest debtor in an economy, will strive towards constant inflation. If one wants a monetary system without any single party being favored, one can have neither inflation nor deflation. The supply of currency must remain constant. This is not achievable with special interest groups meddling in state currencies. It appears more sensible to allow currencies to compete with each other instead.

Recap

- Non-financial corporate debt has increased to unsustainable levels in many countries across the world.
- State deficits must be avoided.
- John Maynard Keynes has had an immense negative influence on modern economic thought.
- The whole banking system is inherently volatile.
- The banking system functions on claims being successfully serviced.
- Capital is becoming more important than human labor in the twenty-first century.
- Inflation and deflation are both bad for special interest groups. Inflation, however, is much worse for the majority of people today.
- Without the act of saving, wealth cannot be created sustainably.

9. Problems and solutions

The old-age provision provided by the state is no longer appropriate in the twenty-first century. To combat this, households must accumulate more productive assets and decrease non-productive and risky assets, such as pension funds and life insurance. As life expectancy increases, so must the retirement age. Because the current median life expectancy in most First World countries is closer to 80 than 65, most people should work until at least that age, unless they can retire on their own investments earlier or receive support from their family. The main goal of the broad population should be to remove all household debt as fast as possible. Once debt-free, the population must accumulate investments to live off in the future. Because it will likely take a few years until appropriate artificial superintelligence starts becoming a reality, there is still enough time to build investments that can supplement one's lifestyle.

Part-time employment on the rise

In many social democracies, as productivity increased over time, instead of working more to fully take advantage of the increased productivity, the mean population worked less. Part-time employment is rising[140], while the average hours worked per year are falling[141]. The role of employment is shifting from being a necessity to being an optional supplement to state welfare. This behavior is unsustainable in the twenty-first century, where many intergenerational institutions fail. Instead, the twenty-first century will be the century of self-preservation for many—working less in this situation is typically quite inappropriate. The working opportunities people will be presented with in the coming decades will be highly paid but will present more weekly working hours than the current standard, since one will have to compete with a combination of artificial superintelligence, machine learning, and robotics. There will be few, if any, working opportunities, even for those willing to work for compensation. On average, though, the working hours will fall even lower than they have previously. This might necessitate a new approach to money. In an unregulated market, artificial intelligence and robotics would lead to little more than an inconvenience at first before increasing the standard of living dramatically and noticeably. The decades of welfare institutions have skewed the market to such a horrid degree that it seems unlikely that the mean population will retain its standard of living, at least in the first half of the twenty-first century.

---

140   *OECD Part-time employment rate (indicator) (2023).*
141   *OECD Hours worked (indicator) (2023).*

IMMIGRATION

Although long-term population predictions are difficult and unlikely to be fully correct, current trends do predict that, excluding most parts of Africa and Southern Asia, the rest of the world will see little population growth in the coming century[142]. As such, politicians have alluded to the idea of using immigration to fix all the problems of demographic change. Even though immigration can affect a welfare system positively, the immigrants must earn at least as much money as the native people for this to plan out properly. This means that the immigrants must be qualified and also work in high-paying positions. Immigration from the most popular asylum-seeking origin countries, on the other hand, has a negative effect on welfare systems.

On average, immigrants have a higher unemployment rate, earn less money, and have higher chances of falling into poverty[143]. As working opportunities in the low-paying sector become less common in the coming decades and the welfare systems fail permanently, many immigrants will have to either fully integrate and still have a small chance of finding employment in high-paying positions. Alternatively, they will have to go back to their countries of origin because welfare money will become more scarce than previously. Because even high-paying positions will become scarce as humans fail

---

142   *United Nations* (2022).
143   BT-Drs. 20/7665, 4f.

to compete with the more productive machines of the twenty-first century, this might lead to a situation where native people try to compete with immigrants for employment, leading to an even more fractured population and possibly increased nationalistic tendencies, which never amount to anything positive. It is problematic that most of those non-western immigrants also have specific countries in mind when they leave their country of origin, usually because of economic inadequacies in their own country. It should be of upmost importance to all social democracies to screen immigrants more effectively and distinguish true political asylum seekers from people who come merely to get free money instead of living in their own country, where the standard of living is lower and they might have to work. Because of the welfare systems in social democracy, the borders have to be locked down at all times. One simply cannot have a welfare system and relatively open borders.

Immigration from incompatible countries must be the exception, not the norm, since they are an objective burden on the system of welfare institutions. If the state does not have a welfare system, those immigrants entering the country enter because they want to work. Immigration control can therefore be much more lax, as seen in the early history of the United States. Because the opposite is true in social democracies, the standard assumption about immigrants entering a country must be that they enter because of the welfare system. This holds especially true when political asylum-seekers from supposedly war-ridden countries do not flee into countries in their near proximity. Instead, they set off on a long journey across the world and the continents, typically paying human traffickers along the way, simply to enter a social democracy. Without some non-governmental organizations providing aid to human traffickers, smugglers, and immigrants, large-scale immigration into western countries would fail after a short while.

Most of the migrants come to Europe because of poor economic situations in their own countries. Few flee their countries because of war or political persecution. Governments of surrounding, more culturally compatible countries could assume responsibility and take on the burden of mass migration, but they either do not or the migrants decide not to enter those countries in the first place. The European Union has facilitated the international human trafficking sector by providing the member countries with secondary law that is incapable of solving even the most basic immigration problems. The poor attempts at immigration built on European solidarity still exist because most of those people working in the high EU institutions are not affected by the mass immigration. They earn large sums of money and live and work in areas and districts that are mostly unaffected by the results of incompatible immigration that fragments the population. It is evident that no state has its important buildings and workplaces in low-income districts. But even many native people living under social democratic governments are willing to live off welfare. The idea of doing so is becoming increasingly alluring, especially to those working in low-paying employment, those with low work morale, and those who are fed up with getting a large portion of their income taken away every time they do earn something. The stigma of receiving government money is vanishing and is becoming fashionable as a lifestyle choice. Welfare recipients nowadays live more comfortably than kings in the Middle Ages and even better than many people in the first half of the twentieth century. They have access to fresh, running water and food. They can light and heat their room on demand and enjoy electricity as well as the internet. Additionally, they have a higher life expectancy than people who lived just half a century ago, have access to more variety in food, and do not need to worry about their children dying at young ages because of diseases that are preventable today. Social democracies have given humanity none of these inventions and improvements to life but are able to distribute them at leisure because of the unfathomable quantity of money flowing into the responsible institutions and agencies.

Welfare unsustainable

In addition to immigration, there are two other options for trying to save the social-equality welfare complex.

Both seem tempting but would partly delegitimize social democratism for the social democratic voter block, which strongly profits from the government safety net. Raising the retirement age and increasing the requirements and conditions that have to be met to receive welfare are unpopular with social democrats. They want the exact opposite, demanding even lower retirement ages or even a universal basic income. Ever since government retirement pensions were introduced in social democratic countries, life expectancy has increased dramatically in the meantime. Yet, the retirement age has not been raised substantially, if at all, under any social democratic government.

On the contrary, many social democrats have proposed lowering the retirement age, although the financial burden is already so heavy that few people can retire on their savings and investments alone. One might assume that to balance the deficit in private retirement investments, the government would encourage private investments to offset the burden on governments. Any progression in that direction is futile, though, as it would mean defeat for the social democratic system. The social democrats would have to acknowledge that their collective system of government welfare is inferior to decentralized provision, saving, and investing that millions of independent people engage in. Due to the intense demographic changes affecting most people today, most pensions are unstable, and many countries require retirees to pay taxes on their pensions. Certain governments even use debt or additional tax money to offset the large deficits that have accumulated over the past few decades. As life expectancy increases, the younger generations have to bear the load of a dying system that they will most likely never profit from themselves. The social systems result in major conflicts of interest that polarize net taxpayers and recipients. Describing this type of financing as social or inducive to equality truly requires a twisted economic perception.

Because in the future, people will live off their investments more frequently, high taxes and mandatory contributions severely inhibit the ability of many to retire on their own. When most people live off investments, exceptionally few people will work at all, due to automation, robotics, and artificial superintelligence becoming cheaper and more able-bodied. In that sense, a natural loss of work through productivity gain is positive, while an artificial loss of work by luring people with welfare and government safety nets into becoming not just less productive but living at the expense of the few remaining productive people is negative. Retiring is a natural process that does not necessarily happen with old age but because people use their productivity to save and invest money in the long term. The government Ponzi scheme system cannot be taken as a proper solution since it is built on deception and fraudulent thinking that benefits previous generations disproportionately compared to later generations.

As people become more productive, retirement ages should fall. However, the opposite must happen today under governments with welfare and safety nets. The retirement ages are rising, and the benefits are decreasing. While, in the short term, many people love forced centralized safety nets because they provide a false sense of security, in the long term, they turn out disastrous. Because the money is not being invested in productive assets, the system requires a constantly working population and forced payments from all citizens. Spending all the generated money immediately will never generate any wealth. Compounding state currency is already harder than it should be. No one personally grows wealthier through constant consumption and spending, despite what some economists claim. Only once someone saves money can the cycle of consumption be broken and wealth be generated.

But not only the current investments are important. Inheritances are the most essential basis for building sustainable wealth over multiple generations. If all wealth and capital were destroyed every time someone died, the whole population would have to be rebuilt every generation. In social democracies, people are taxed even for dying and passing on their wealth to their families. People who can uphold and grow wealth are a danger to social democracies because they are at risk of becoming fully independent of the government.

Creating capital and wealth is hard; keeping and growing that wealth in the family for one generation is even harder, but only a tiny number of people can keep and grow wealth over many generations. With every generation, more people come into contact with the family's wealth, and it becomes harder to maintain, especially if family members are financially illiterate. In the present, many people have chosen not to let their families inherit a part of their wealth. Instead, they live a hedonistic life of overspending. The fact that many people in fiscally irresponsible social democratic countries with large debt-to-GDP ratios have debt themselves is not a coincidence. Thus, high time preference on the government's side meet a similar high time preference on the side of its subordinates.

Universal Basic Income

An increasing portion of the population believes that reforming the government safety net would solve the many bad aspects of safety nets. They call it universal basic income. It is a contemporary socialist attempt to strengthen the bond between the government and the receiving citizen while further weakening the relationship between the state and its paying citizen. As the name suggests, a universal basic income proposes that, universally in the population, a basic monetary supplement, previously determined by the government as high enough to live on, is distributed by said government and paid for by tax revenue and debt. Minimum wages are the first step towards a universal basic income.

The flawed logic of income equality comes from extrapolating equality onto every aspect of human nature, stripping the human from said nature in the process. This egalitarian state is the social democratic utopia and should remind the reader of the attempts and ideas to establish a utopia that socialists have made over the centuries, as discussed in previous chapters. Typically, proponents of UBI have three main reasons why they believe it to be superior to contemporary government safety nets. The first assumption is that it will never provide ample money to comfortably live on, and thus, people will be more inclined to work for more money. This is a flawed argument, as universal basic income discourages work beyond a certain threshold. Under the threshold, which will vary from population to population, it makes people more inclined to lower their standard of living or work jobs merely to supplement the UBI, not the other way around. If the payment is too low, this would additionally undermine the social democratic idea of redistributing money and wealth.

The argument in favor of UBI presupposes that people want to work to uphold their current standard of living. This is unrealistic, especially in today's environment, in which employees are more likely to become sick or experience burnout. When presented with the opportunity to slightly scale down their standard of living in exchange for the ability to work less or not at all, many will gladly make that sacrifice if it means being able to have more free time or spend more time with their family and friends, all while having their endeavor financed by a third party.

The second reason behind the idea is that redistributing money among a population creates more equality than before. This is a typical social democratic error that has a long history and can be traced back to original socialist thought. Any population whose inhabitants all have an equal amount of money will still behave differently. Some will spend it all in a short period of time. Others might save most of it. Constantly redistributing the money so that those who spent the money get more money at the expense of people with low time preferences is certainly not equal and does not encourage responsible finances.

Proponents of UBI also believe that it reduces bureaucracy because it would replace all government social systems. Due to its universal nature, there are no specific applications, as everyone receives the supplement regardless of income. This may be true, but social democratic governments are unable to reduce bureaucracy without increasing it elsewhere because they constantly expand their endeavors. Financing the UBI is impossible without also increasing the effective tax burden on net-productive persons even further, which seems politically unfeasible. The tolerance for confiscation is different for everyone, but most people seem to tolerate up to fifty percent immediate income loss, excluding the tax burden from all other forms of taxation, both direct and indirect.

Some social democracies are dangerously close to that threshold in certain financial constellations, and will have to increase tax rates, or the tax base for those in lower tax brackets, if they wish to distribute the burden of UBI equally. It appears that many politicians are aware that their institutionalized social system can no longer be properly financed. Regardless, it seems like they are still trying to ride the sinking ship, each wanting a piece of the cake, until ultimately the cake sinks into the water, becomes soggy, and slowly dissolves, just like their system. It will be interesting to see how the social democratic elitists will try to solve this problem.

HUMANS WANT TO ESTABLISH STATES

It is a human desire to establish governments, be it in small tribes, in the form of one leader, or in larger civilizations, as entire parliaments and millions of civil servants work at the cost of those paying taxes. Even food and water are taxed, so everyone is a taxpayer. There is no escape, and there is no voluntary association with alternatives. The totality of civil servants somehow equates to public service. However, the public does not decide this; the state is the one to decide who is deemed to be of service to the public[144].

This creates a situation in which the state projects its own desire for civil servants onto the population. The term public service also implies that civil servants are somehow not part of the public. If they were, they would serve themselves, thereby defeating the purpose of service. An easy way of effectively reducing the number of civil servants is to use competing contractors to fill in positions that would have otherwise been occupied by the supposedly secure jobs of decade-long positions in the state sector. Although the contractors would also work for the state, the positions are limited by contracts and based on performance. If the contractor is not needed anymore or performs poorly, he is discarded or replaced without commitments to pensions or job security. Reducing the number of pensioners also allows the state to focus on higher-paying positions within the state that fill critical roles. This is especially important in the twenty-first century, which sees a shift away from the service sector to one in which a few highly paid specialists might be able to increase their productivity beyond that of automation capabilities. At least in the next few decades. It is widely known that the state sector is often the last to adopt vital technologies. This further increases the chance of a total state default in the

---

144   *Sowell* (1995), 184.

upcoming decades. When the state has to inevitably reduce the number of civil servants, many will find themselves to only be qualified for work in the state sector while only having little investment of their own because of the inherent trust in the penstion system. It is evident now that an alternative system must be conceived soon.

No social democratic government would ever allow such an alternative system to exist, however, since it has the potential to severely limit state power. As long as there are people in governments profiting from social democracy, the probability of such an overhaul is close to zero, without any external intervention. Governments naturally grow in power and influence without explicitly asking every one of their citizens for permission, as it is presumed to be too difficult. That being said, in this world, which includes multinational companies with millions of customers, this way of thinking is highly questionable. Especially with respect to the technological possibilities and advancements in the twenty-first century that easily allow for extensive customer relationship management systems to be established.

The author proposes an alternative system of truly absolute property rights. At the same time, the paternalism of social democracies many have grown accustomed to needs to be preserved in some shape or form, unless one wishes for violent protests. Because social democratism upholds a twisted form of the consent of the governed, elections must no longer ensue to fix this issue. Instead, consent to being governed can be achieved through simple terms, conditions, and contracts. States should not be any different in that respect, although it might take time to adjust. The goal is to offer individual service for every citizen. All government services should be able to be individually opted out of. The voluntary and personal aspect of building one's own government, entirely within a contract, allows for much more choice, representation, and decision-making than mere voting. The state services could be used according to one's state subscription and contract. Not only does this system allow younger and older people to use services according to their specific needs, but it also respects the dynamic living situation of twenty-first-century people.

Upholding the right to property means upholding the right to life and the right to liberty simultaneously. Everyone owns his or her body; in that sense, you are your own property. Without these three rights, the individual is no longer a free human. Anything or anyone trying to alienate these rights, be it by force from governments, militant groups, or any illegitimate contract, is void and non-binding if one upholds absolute property rights. History has established that humans cannot be trusted to uphold such a theoretical framework themselves. Humans in positions of power will exploit their power in some shape or form. Artificial superintelligence is the only realistic and future-proof option for upholding a framework that could potentially be relatively independent of human subjectivity. In a few decades, artificial intelligence will be more than qualified to keep humans in check and ensure the objectives are being followed. There is an inherent danger emanating from artificial intelligence if humans start to abuse it and exploit its power. For that reason alone, making sure that the three natural human rights are protected at all times should be the main goal in this framework.

The framework does not need government branches because it establishes and maintains only three rights. It stands above governments and does not try to emulate them. Any form of government can be allowed under a framework of freedom if it respects the three natural rights of humans: life, liberty, and property. It is therefore important to differentiate between legitimate governments, established using contracts between the government and all its citizens, and illegitimate and unjust governments, purely upheld through coercion, intimidation, and force. If someone does decide to leave a government system or institution, he or she naturally voids all benefits associated with the institution or might have the option to get a specific sum paid out if money was involved. Just like with any other contract, voiding the contract must be a viable option, even if it means facing seemingly harsh consequences. Allowing everyone to live as they please is crucial if human civilization wants to break the cycle of destruction caused by forced governments. This framework could be implemented easily once artificial intelligence, robotics, and automation become advanced enough, but it causes governments to lose control and is therefore a purely utopian concept that, for now, can only be conceived if artificial intelligence becomes more powerful. Humanity is far from artificial intelligence enforcing the set rules of conduct in the framework proposed here, and the thought of such a framework, as unlikely as it might be, is still more realistic than humanity ever agreeing on one political system.

Unlike in governments, this framework does not use human legislators, who live off constantly creating new legislation and updating established legislation. Legislation is unproblematic, as long as it does not cause the three natural laws to be voided. Artificial intelligence should not use legislation to prevent subjective decision-making from occurring; it should only use it to remove subjectivity that harms other people's freedom. The natural body of decision-making cannot be artificially stunted, as seen under social democratic legislation, and should be restored to ensure that people can make all decisions by themselves if they wish to do so. The government can continue operating its institutions and systems, provided it finances them legitimately. Everyone can leave the institutions and systems and use the competing services if they happen to be superior. Knowing that civilizations thrive in times of peace more so than in times of war and conflict, it does beg the question of why, in today's age of artificial intelligence, the idea of governments, in turn, being governed by this power, is not discussed on a wider scale. For obvious reasons, any governing authority commanded by artificial superintelligence, that is able to confidently keep governments in check is still a few decades away, but it is also a realistic option in the future that should not be disregarded immediately. Although there has been discourse about the possibility of a government consisting of artificial intelligence, that aspect does not keep governments in check; it merely replaces them. That does not solve the issue since it would encourage human governments to establish their own primacy again and banish or destroy artificial intelligence, thereby restarting the whole cycle from the beginning.

Before establishing a proper governing authority for governments, trying to replace the core of social democratism is the easiest way to accelerate the decay of this destructive ideology. Some changes can be made to improve the lives of people living under social democratism. Because most solutions require the government to change, they really are not more than wishful thinking. The only true help one has to combat social democratism is education. Keeping the dying liberal values alive and letting them prosper despite the adverse conditions is all one can do. By participating in charities and organizations that work towards particular goals, one can ensure that the influence in certain areas of life is taken away from the monopoly of the state. Local organizations and charities can aid and assist people more efficiently than the state ever could. The church runs many almsgiving programs around the world and finances itself through donations and voluntary contributions—at least in the United States[145]. There is no argument to be made against a welfare system established on donations and voluntary reoccurring contributions. Any violence against the state or coup d'état is futile because it would either result in civil war or another social democratic government—just a different one. Therefore, the author distances himself from such operations and endeavors and admonishes the reader to use stoic moderation and logical reasoning instead of violence.

IDEAL GOVERNMENT

What constitutes an ideal government? Although most uneducated people today would say democracy and, in the same sentence, demonize all other elements of a republic, historic reality teaches us that taking elements of monarchy and aristocracy is the only way of ensuring a stable state. In the system of aristocracy, the aristocrats are bound by their own decisions and legislation. In a limited monarchy, the monarch does not have absolute power, which is satisfactory—the goal here is to limit power. When combining two

---

145   *Uhle (ed.)/Haering (2015)*, 33.

representative monarchs with veto rights, who are bound by natural law, and an aristocratic council that is bound by the monarchs' veto rights and the law, the system becomes even more ideal. The monarch acts only as a representative but must use his veto right against legislation passed by the aristocratic council that violates natural law. This ensures that the population is never subjected to penalizing legislation in any form. This removes the need for a politicized democratic parliament, subject to populism and lobbying. It is important, however, that the aristocrats in the legislative branch do not have any prerogatives compared to the mean population.

The democratic state does not value persistent leadership, such as in a company or a monarchy. It does, however, consider the state employees to be the persistent part of the state. The pension becomes a tool to guarantee their impartiality and moral fortitude against change in government[146]. This presupposes that the civil servants experience a selfless love of the state, as seen in those state employees of past monarchies. In reality, civil servants are barely different from the mean working population, who simply want an opportunity to earn money. The main difference between state employees and employees in a market is that they do not have to worry about having their employment terminated, unlike those in the market. Although the risk

---

146   *Domizlaff* (1957), 219f.

is greater in the market, so is the potential for reward. People who oppose hereditary monarchism must also oppose the hereditary consent of constitutions. Therefore, every person born into the state must be able to consent to the constitution (terms and conditions). He may later choose to secede from the country. Since, at this point, the state is a competing organization, it has an inherent interest in gaining members. Further details would be thought of by the individual organizations. Peaceful competition between states could then create a multitude of systems. Anything in the political range could exist, provided the people consent to it and have the ability to secede. This system would reduce the hegemonial position of social democracy but not inherently hinder the existence of social democracies.

The Ancient Roman *cursus honorum* established that magistrates were only able to hold their position for one year, without the option to be reelected for the same position again. The magistrates also had to wait two years between positions, so the government employees were unable to stay in their positions permanently. To have the ability to control the power of the magistrate, the civil servants were never in positions alone. Even the highest position, the consul, had two people bearing the office, both having a right to veto the other's decision. Only the best became civil servants—a guiding principle that defined the position of the civil servant for centuries, well into the nineteenth century, until governments reformed the position into being suitable for the masses and started massively increasing the number of civil servants.

LIMITING STATE-QUOTA

For most social democracies, the state quota surpassed fifteen percent during or after World War I. The United States managed to hold out until World War II[147]. In order to stabilize state finances, government revenue as a percent of GDP must be capped at a sensible rate, such as one percent, if the previous idea does not manifest itself. Although this might seem like a low rate, using the 2022 GDP of the United States, the state would still receive over 200 billion dollars, which is enough to secure the judicial branch of the government, the police, and uphold a small but effective military. Because the majority of the costs associated with these branches of government are salaries, automation and robotics might be able to alleviate large portions of the employment, once artificial superintelligence has matured enough as a concept and technology. Allowing governments to exist at all reduces the risk that potential militant groups will come to power and act like pseudo-governments themselves. Governments will not be able to be forbidden as long as humans continue to live on this planet. The ideal population that outgrows its necessity for the state might exist in the distant future but will probably not comprise humans. Allowing voluntary

---

147   International Monetary Fund (2022).

association with anything government-related, just like in all other aspects of life, is the only way of peacefully achieving a semi-harmonious state of living, where those with opposing opinions and differing conceptions of reality do not constantly clash together unless they do so on purpose. This allows everyone, regardless of opinion, to live and thrive, as long as the person does not inhibit others in their life, liberty, or property.

The state becomes a corporation

To further expand on the ideal version of the modern state of the twenty-first century, is to imagine a state that is managed like a company, with shareholder meetings (voluntary elements), a board of directors (aristocracy), and a CEO (monarchy). The law must be based on natural law, merely supplemented with legislation. Most legislation can be replaced by an efficient interpretation of the constitution using artificial intelligence. All interpretations must pass the strict layer of natural law. This provides a proper foundation for a new legal state based on a combination of civil law and common law. Further democratic elements must perish, as they become worthless in a state of law. The state can provide services, enterprise, and compete with other companies for customers. It has little authority to begin with, but it must stay profitable. If the state becomes a corporation, then the citizens can agree to fees and contributions. Similar to modern streaming services, the individual must be able to withdraw from the service if he wishes to. Similarly, all additional burden in the form of mandatory insurance and social institution costs must be reduced until they no longer comprise any part of the state's revenue; insurance and welfare must be optional. This can be achieved by allowing people to forfeit their claim against the state in exchange for not having to pay into the system. At the same time, the state must be restructured. Although insolvency is not a real threat, due to the monopoly on currency, the effects of saving the state from temporarily being unable to pay short-term obligations through monetary measures do affect the population negatively. In a future population of primarily unemployed people, the goal must be to establish a wide class of the so-despised rentiers. The alternative is a wide-spread reduction of wealth and the possibility of large percentiles of the population becoming economically impoverished.

SHAREHOLDER MEETINGS

To combat this, just as only shareholders in companies can make decisions, the same should be applied to the government. Only those paying can be part of the shareholder meetings and decide on the fate of the company. Equal voting rights at shareholder meetings are fully implausible, since some people own more stock than others. No logical and rational argument can deny that this system of voting relative to participation is inherently more just than allowing everyone to vote on the fate of the company, regardless of actual involvement in the company. Democratic shareholder meetings would result in everyone being allowed to vote in every shareholder meeting, whether one owns one percent of the shares, ten percent, or nothing at all. In this democratized concept of shareholder voting, similar to that proposed by the ideology of stakeholder capitalism, the market can no longer function properly. Through their equalized votes, people could overrule even those who risk the most by having given the most equity to the company in question. The author therefore proposes a system of a voluntary, equity-based, shareholder state. Everyone willing to buy parts of the state would hold equity in it. This, in turn, would result in certain claims against the state. The state could be a large holding company with multiple subsidiaries, each responsible for different functions. Because everyone willing to buy a part of the state must also be a member of the state, but not vice versa, this means that those with influence will only be those who are citizens (shareholders).

This construction is also less likely to increase state debts since the consensus on doing so is harder and affects every shareholder's equity negatively. In such a hypothetical state, even billionaires would not hold the majority interest since they could use their wealth more effectively in the market. The broad population in social democracies, collectively, has implicit claims against the state, usually amounting to trillions of units of currency. If those claims against the current social democracies could be switched to shareholder equity through a debt-equity swap, the state could use the new equity to finance its endeavors by competing in the market with other companies that can profit from the increased technological productivity. Just like any other public company, the state organization would have to commit to double-entry accounting and abolish, at least, taxation and the currency monopoly. Because the transition into an economy of scarce employment will take years, even when the needed technology is already available, the social democratic states must act in the present; they cannot afford to wait any longer. Because some governments do not allow pensions to be part of debt-equity swaps, legislation would have to be changed accordingly to allow more autonomy in that regard. Until the transition into the new economy is completed, it is best for all economic actors to earn money excessively while living in austerity. This is the only way that sustainable investments can be built by the broad population, no matter their income.

This, however, is only possible when the state reduces its services and, thereby, its costs and revenue at the same time. If this is not done soon, the only option for the mean population will be to increase consumer debt. Because the current claims against the state, in the form of implicit debt, will likely never be properly repaid, it is in the interest of the population that the welfare system be replaced with equity-based ownership of the state. Claims against state-run welfare institutions are neither secure nor guaranteed to be high enough to live off in the future. When the state is not in a position to accumulate any more debt, the claim against the state might not even be enforceable. The alternative is ownership as a shareholder in the state. As a shareholder, one is providing the state with the necessary liquidity to establish profitable companies and compete in the market. If the concept of the nation-state stays static for any longer, the present issues will completely devour what is left of social democracy in the next few decades.

Social democratism is unsustainable

As previously established in the book, like any socialist idea of government, social democratism is an unsustainable and dying utopian concept unfit for the modern world. It will not be able to prevail in the twenty-first century without giving up substantial parts of its ideology. Socialism is deeply engrained in the ideology, as established by one of the creators of the social democratic movement[148], who admits that socialism and democratism complement each other. Although the idea of compromises between socialism and liberalism is less radical than other forms of radical socialism, such as scientific socialism or national

---

148   *Liebknecht* (2012), 276.

socialism, it still suffers from the same errors that inevitably led to the downfall of all socialist experiments in the past. Allowing bits and pieces of liberal ideology to pass into the system merely lengthens the lifespan of a social democracy. The important question one has to ask is not if this system will fail in the twenty-first century, but rather what system succeeds social democratism. Such a system must be one of great compromises, but one that still decides in favor of liberalism.

RECAP

- Claims against the state and its welfare institutions are implicit debt.
- Because humans might no longer be competitive enough in the future, fewer employment opportunities will be available.
- By using debt-equity swaps on the claims that citizens have against the welfare institutions of the state, the welfare system could be saved.
- The state could be managed like a joint-stock company.
- The state must become a profitable organization.
- The state can use customer relationship management systems to manage the consent of its citizens.

REFERENCE LIST

2023 Edelman Trust Barometer, 8-11.

Ahiakpor, James C. W. (1995). A paradox of thrift or Keynes misrepresentation of saving in the classical theory of growth? Southern Economic Journal, 62(1), 16–33 (17, 19, 28f).

AMECO (autumn 2022).

Auerbach, Alan J. (1987). Taxation of Income. *The Palgrave Dictionary of Economics.* Palgrave Macmillan, 1.

Bank of International Settlements (2023). Credit to the non-financial sector. https://data.bis.org/topics/TOTAL_CREDIT.

Banken, R. (2018). Hitlers Steuerstaat: Die Steuerpolitik im Dritten Reich. De Gruyter Oldenbourg, 404–408. 414, 32, 34, 36, 357 https://doi.org/10.1515/9783486992649.

Bastiat, Frédéric/Cain, Seymour (transl.)/de Huszar, George B. (ed.) (1995). *Selected essays on political economy.* Foundation for Economic Education, 272.

Bastiat, Frédéric/Sterling, Patrick James (transl.) (1850/1891). *The law.* Demetra, 18.

Biersack, Heinrich Ludwig (1850). *Über Besteuerung, ihre Grunsätze und ihre Ausführung.* Verlag Heinrich Ludwig Brönner, 98.

Bookchin, M. (1998). The Third Revolution: Popular Movements in the Revolutionary Era. Volume 2.

Wiltshire: Redwood Books, 278, 279.

Brenke, K. (2009). Reallöhne in Deutschland über mehrere Jahre rückläufig. Wochenbericht des DIW Berlin Nr. 33/2009, 550-560.

Bry, G. (1960). Wages in Germany 1871-1945. Princeton University Press, 467.

Burlamaqui, Jean-Jaques/Nugent, Thomas (transl.)/Korkman, Petter (ed.) (1752/2006). *The priciples of natural and political law.* Liberty Fund, 64.

Burnham, James (1943). *The Machiavellians: defenders of freedom.* Lume Books, 128f.

von Böhm-Bawerk, Eugen (1896/2016). *Zum Abschluss des Marxschen Systems.* Oeconimus, 75f.

Cantillon, Richard/Murphy, Antoin E. (ed.) (1734/2015). Essay on the nature of trade in general. Liberty Fund, 56.

Christlich Demokratische Union. (1946). Parteiprogramm von Neheim-Hüsten (1.3.1946). (n.p.), 5.

Christlich Demokratische Union. (1947). CDU überwindet Kapitalismus und Marxismus: Das Ahlener Wirtschafts- und Sozialprogramm der CDU und die Grundlegenden Anträge der CDU im Landtag von Nordrhein-Westfalen. Heiderdruck Bergisch Gladbach, 3.

Constant, Bejamin/O`Keeffe, Dennis.(transl.). *Principles of politics applicable to all governments.* Liberty Fund, 96.

Credit Suisse/UBS (2023). *Global Wealth Databook 2023*, 26.

Das Eisenacher Programm: beschlossen auf dem Parteitag des Allgemeinen Deutschen sozialdemokratischen Arbeiterkongresses zu Eisenach am 7., 8. und 9. August 1869. (1947). *Sozialistische Dokumente: Schriftenreihe Demokratie und Sozialismus Heft 6.* Bollwerk-Verlag Karl Drott, 121.

Davies, J.B., Lluberas, R. and Shorrocks, A.F. (2017), Estimating the Level and Distribution of Global Wealth, 2000–2014. *Review of Income and Wealth* 63, 731-759(757). https://doi.org/10.1111/roiw.12318.

De Molinari, Gustave (1849). From the production of security. *Journal of Economists,* vol. 22, 278.

Delsol, Jean-Philippe (ed.)/Lecaussin, Nicolas (ed.)/Martin, Emmanuel (ed.) et al. (2017). *Anti-Piketty: capital for the twenty-first century.* Cato Institute, 94.

Domizlaff, Hans (1957). *Die Seele des Staates: Regelbuch der Elite.* (n.p.), 219f.

Draper, T. (1972). The specter of Weimar. Social Research, 39(2), 335.

Drumetz, Françoise/Pfister, Christian (2021). Modern monetary theory: a wrong compass for decision-making. *Intereconomics* 56, 355–361(358). https://doi.org/10.1007/s10272-021-1014-5.

Engels, F., Marx, K. (1848). *Manifest der kommunistischen Partei: veröffentlicht im Februar 1848.* Bildungs-Gesellschaft für Arbeiter, 16.

EUROSTAT (2023). Real GDP per capita [sdg_08_10].

Freiherr von Pufendorf, S./Breslau, H. (1667/1870). *Über die Verfassung des deutschen Reichs.* MV-History, 92f.

Fremdling, Rainer (1980). Freight rates and state budget: the role of the national prussian railways 1880–1913. *The journal of european economic history vol. 9, 21–39(32).*

Fritze, Lothar (2012). *Anatomie des totalitären Denkens:*

kommunistische und nationalsozialistische Weltanschauung im Vergleich. Olzog, 183f.

Fuller, Edward W. (2019). Keynes and the Ethics of Socialism *Quarterly Journal of Austrian Economics, 22(2):* 139–180(145) https://doi.org/10.35297/qjae.010010.

Genovese, Frederica/Scheve, Kenneth/Stasavage, David (2016). *Comparative Income Taxation Database.* https://data.stanford.edu/citd (last accessed Dec. 2023).

Goebbels, J. (1932). *„Der Nazi-Sozi" Fragen und Antworten für den Nationalsozialisten.* Verlag der Nationalsozialistischen Briefe, 15.

Goodhart, Charles/Pradhan, Manoj (2020). *The great demographic reversal: ageing societies, waning inequality, and an inflation revival.* Palgrave macmillan, 197.

Green, Nancy (1985). Socialist anti-semitism, defense of a bourgeois jew and discovery of the jewish proletariat: changing attitudes of french socialists before 1914. *International Review of Social History, 30*(3), 374–399 (381f.). doi:10.1017/S0020859000111666.

Harper, David A./Endres, Anthony M. (2022). Menger's precursors in the german subjective-value tradition and his advancements in the theory of wants and goods. *The Review of Austrian Economics 36,* 217–245(222). https://doi.org/10.1007/s11138-022-00598-5.

von Hayek, Friedrich August/Bartley III, William Warren (ed.) (1988). *The fatal conceit: the errors of socialism.* Chicago University Press, 114.

Hazlitt, Henry (1965). Confusion, not conspiracy. *National Review,* June 1, 1965, 468f.

Henry, L. A., & Douhovnikoff, V. (2008). Environmental Issues in Russia. Annual Review of Environment and Resources, 33(1), 438. http://doi.org/10.1146/annurev.environ.33.0510 07.082437.

Hirschburger, Adolf (ed.) (1923). *Einkommensteuergesetz vom 29. März 1920: Unter Berücksichtigung der bis zum 23. Dezember 1922 ergangenen Änderungs- und Ergänzungsgesetze.* Walter de Gruyter, 185.

Hitler, A. (1925/1927). Mein Kampf: Zwei Bände in einem Band: Ungekürzte Ausgabe. Franz Eher Nachf. Verlag, 590.

Hochschild, Udo (2022). *Engel Menschen Gewaltenteilung: Realität eines Verfassungsprinzips.* Atticus, 26.

International Monetary Fund (2022). *Government revenue, percent of GDP* in: Public Finances in Modern History Database (Dec 2022).

International Monetary Fund (2023). *General government gross debt: percent of GDP* in: World Economic Outlook (October 2023).

Keynes, John Maynard (1931/2010). *Essays in Persuasion.* palgrave macmillan, 299.

Keynes, John Maynard (1931/2010). *Essays in Persuasion.* palgrave macmillan, 64, 67.

Keynes, John Maynard (1931/2010). *Essays in Persuasion.* palgrave macmillan, 75.

Ritter von Kuehnelt-Leddihn, E. (1952). Liberty or Equality: The Challenge of our Time. Caxton Printers, 281.

Ritter von Kuehnelt-Leddihn, E. (1972, November). The Roots of Anticapitalism. *The Freeman, 22*(11), 658.

Ritter von Kuehnelt-Leddihn, E. (1985/2019). *Gleichheit*

oder Freiheit?: Demokratie – ein babylonischer Turmbau. Ares Verlag, 324f.

Larenz, Karl/Canaris, Claus-Wilhelm (1995). *Methodenlehre der Rechtswissenschaft.* Springer Verlag, 25, 28.

Leoni, Bruno/ Kemp, Arthur (ed.) (1961/1991). *Freedom and the law.* Liberty Fund, 236.

Liebknecht, W. (2012). Kleine politische Schriften. Tredition, 276.

Locke, John (1689/1884) *Two treatises on civil government.* Routledge, 234f.

Locke, John (1689/1884) *Two treatises on civil government.* Routledge, 261f.

Lüdemann, Peter (2015). *Abgezockt und kaltgestellt: Wie der deutsche Steuerzahler systematisch augeplündert wird.* Finanzbuchverlag, 69, 77, 82.

Makin, Tony/Tunny, Gene (2021). The MMT hoax. *Policy Paper 41.* Centre for Independent Studies, 4.

Maltsev, Juri N (ed.). (1993/2012) *Requiem for Marx.* Ludwig von Mises Insitiute, 8.

Marcuse, H./Kellner, D. (ed.) (2001). *Towards a critical theory of Society: Collected Papers of Herbert Marcuse,* vol. 2. Routledge, 50.

Marx, K. Engels, F. (1888). *Ludwig Feuerbach und der Ausgang der klassischen Deutschen Philosophie: Mit Anhang: Karl Marx über Feuerback vom Jahre 1845.* J. H. W. Dietz, 72.

Marx, K., Engels, F. (1844/1968). *Marx-Engels-Werke,* Bd. 40, Dietz Verlag, 546.

Marx, Karl/Engels, Friedrich (1974). *Werke, Bd. 30.* Dietz Verlag, 257.

Marx, Karl/Engels, Friedrich (1981). *Werke, Bd. 1.* Dietz Verlag, 374f.

Marx, Karl/Engels, Friedrich: *Das Kommunistische*

Manifest. Mit mehreren Anhängen: Die Programme der deutschen sozialistischen Parteien. (1919). Revolutions-Bibliothek Nr. 3. Verlag Gesellschaft und Erziehung, 32.

Matzerath, H., & Turner, H. A. (1977). Die Selbstfinanzierung der NSDAP 1930—1932. *Geschichte Und Gesellschaft, 3*(1), 64, 70. www.jstor.org/stable/40184942.

von Mayenburg, David (ed.) (2021). Handbuch zur Geschichte der Konfliktlösung in Europa. vol. 2. Springer, 454.

Menger, Carl (1871/2022). *Grundsätze der Volkswirtschaftslehre.* Oeconimus, 135.

Mill, John Stuart/Mill, Harriet Taylor/Robson, John (ed.) (1851). *Collected works of John Stuart Mill, vol. 21.* Liberty Fund, 395.

von Mises, Ludwig (1951/2012). *Socialism: an economic and sociological analysis.* Martino publishing, 101.

von Mises, Ludwig Heinrich (1949/2020). *Humans action: a treatise on economics.* Mises Institute, 861.

Moatsos, Michail (2021) Global extreme poverty: Present and past since 1820 in: *How Was Life? Volume II: New Perspectives on Well-being and Global Inequality since 1820.* OECD Publishing, 195. https://doi.org/10.1787/3d96efc5-en.

Morelly, É. (1755/1841). *Code De La Nature.* Paul Masgana, 158, 175.

Mueller, Gustav E. (1958). The hegel legend of "Thesis-Antithesis-Synthesis". *Journal of the History of Ideas, 19(3),* 411–414(413).

NSDAP (1926/2013). Protokoll der Generalmitgliederversammlung der NSDAP/NSDAV e. V. in München. In *Hitler. Quellen 1924–45 Online.* De Gruyter.

www.degruyter.com/database/HITQ/entry/HRSA-0147/html.

NSDAP (1926/2013). Protokoll der Generalmitgliederversammlung der NSDAP/NSDAV e. V. in München. In *Hitler. Quellen 1924–45 Online*. De Gruyter. www.degruyter.com/database/HITQ/entry/HRSA-0488/html.

Nuernberg military tribunals no. 10, vol. 7 (1953), 556, 567f.

OECD (2023), Financial disincentive to increase working hours (indicator). http://doi.org/10.1787/2a7f0afe-en (accessed on 18 November 2023).

OECD (2023), Financial disincentive to return to work (indicator). http://doi.org/10.1787/3ef6e9d7-en (accessed on 04 November 2023).

OECD (2023), *General government deficit (indicator)*. http://doi.org/10.1787/77079edb-en (accessed on 03 November 2023).

OECD (2023), Hours worked (indicator). http://doi.org/10.1787/47be1c78-en (Accessed on 01 December 2023).

OECD (2023), Part-time employment rate (indicator). https://doi.org/10.1787/f2ad596c-en (accessed on 17 November 2023).

OECD (2023), Tax on goods and services (indicator). http://doi.org/10.1787/40b85101-en (accessed on 18 November 2023).

OECD (2023), Tax wedge (indicator).

OECD (2023), Trust in government (indicator). http://doi.org/10.1787/1de9675e-en (accessed on 18 November 2023)

OECD (2023). Labour productivity forecast (indicator)

OECD (2023). Total, US dollars, 1990-2016. Average
      wages (indicator).
      https://doi.org/10.1787/cc3e1387-en
Osoba, L., (1996). The Destruction of the Environment in
      the Former Soviet Union, 5 Dalhousie Journal of
      Legal Studies 167, CanLIIDocs 7, 176.
      https://canlii.ca/t/2889.
Parkinson, Northcote C. (1958). *Parkinson's Law: or the
      pursuit of progress.* John Murray, 10.
Paul, H., Taylor, J., Knight, P. and Marsh, N. (2022).
      Chapter 2. Navigating the Market (1800–1870).
      *Invested: How Three Centuries of Stock Market
      Advice Reshaped Our Money, Markets, and Minds.*
      Chicago: University of Chicago Press, 41.
Petty, William (1662). *A treatise of taxes & contributions,*
      9f.
Piketty, Thomas/Goldhammer, Arthur (transl.) (2014).
      Capital in the twenty-first century. Harvard
      University Press, 499.
Pilbeam, P. (2013). *Saint-Simonians in Nineteenth-
      Century France: From Free Love to Algeria.* Palgrave
      Macmillan, 2.
Popper, K. (1957/1986). *The poverty of historicism.* Ark,
      47.
Popper, K. (1994). *The Open Society and Its Enemies.*
      Princeton University Press, 253.
Proudhon, P. (1848). *Solution du problème social.* Pilhes,
      85.
Quinn, William, Turner, John D. (2020). *Boom and bust: a
      global history of financial bubbles.* Cambridge
      University Press, 138f.
Reichsflaggengesetz vom 15. September 1935
      (RGBl. I S. 1145); Reichsbürgergesetz vom 15.
      September 1935 (RGBl. I S. 1146); Gesetz zum

Schutze des deutschen Blutes und der deutschen Ehre vom 15. September 1935 (RGBl. I S. 1146).

Rockefeller, D. (2003). Memoirs. Random House Trade Paperbacks, 406.

Sahm, Reiner (2018). *Zum Teufel mit der Steuer!: 5000 Jahre Steuern – ein langer Leidensweg der Menschheit.* Springer, 252, 293.

Sahm, Reiner (2023). *Die Entstehung der Einkommensteuer: Eine historische Betrachtung ihrer Anfänge und Entwicklung.* Springer Fachmedien, 4.

Schmidt, M. G., Ostheim, T., Siegel, N. A., Zohlnhöfer, R. (Eds.) (2007). Der Wohlfahrtsstaat: Eine Einführung in den historischen und internationalen Vergleich. VS Verlag für Sozialwissenschaften Wiesbaden, 145. https://doi.org/10.1007/978-3-531-90708-6.

Schnellenbach, Jan (2019). Revisiting the tension between classical liberalism and the welfare state. *Journal of Contextual Economics 139,* 365–384(374).

Schuknecht, L., Tanzi, V. and Afonso, A., (2003). Public sector efficiency: an international comparison (No. 242). European Central Bank, 24.

Smith, Adam/Cannan, Edwin (ed.) (1776/1903). *An inquiry into the nature and causes of the wealth of nations,* vol. 1. Methuen, 71.

Somary, F. (1952). *Krise und Zukunft der Demokratie.* TvR Medienverlag Jena, 147f.

Somary, Felix (1984/2010) *Krise und Zukunft der Demokratie.* TvR Medienverlag, 114.

Sowell, Thomas (1995). *The vision of the annointed: self-congratulation as a basis for social policy.* Basic books, 184.

Sowell, Thomas (2005). *Black rednecks and white liberals*. Encounter Books, 28.

Sozialdemokratische Partei Deutschlands. (1959). *Grundsatzprogramm der Sozialdemokratischen Partei Deutschlands. Beschlossen vom Außerordentlichen Parteitag der Sozialdemokratischen Partei Deutschlands in Bad Godesberg vom 13. bis 15. November 1959*. Vorstand der Sozialdemokratischen Partei Deutschlands, 8.

Sozialdemokratische Partei Deutschlands. (1989/1998). *Grundsatzprogramm der Sozialdemokratischen Partei Deutschlands*, 52.

Sozialdemokratische Partei Deutschlands. (2007). *Hamburger Programm: Grundsatzprogramm der Sozialdemokratischen Partei Deutschlands*, 16f.

Toye, John (1997). Keynes on population and economic growth. *Cambridge Journal of Economics*, vol. 21, 1–26(14).

Trials of war criminals before the Nuernberg military tribunals under control council law no. 10, volume VII. (1953). United States Government Printing Office, 556, 567f.

Turner, Henry Ashby (1985). *German big business and the rise of Hitler*. Oxford University Press, 114, 341.

Uhle, Arnd (ed.)/Haering, Stephan (2015). *Kirchenfinanzen in der Diskussion: Aktuelle Fragen der Kirchenfinanzierung und der kirchlichen Vermögensverwaltung*. Duncker & Humblot, 33.

Ullmann, Hans-Peter (2005). *Der deutsche Steuerstaat; Geschichte der öffentlichen Finanzen vom 18. Jahrhundert bis heute*. C.H Beck, 50.

United Nations, Department of Economic and Social Affairs, Population Division (2022). *World Population Prospects 2022: Summary of Results*. UN

DESA/POP/2022/TR/NO. 3., 29.

van der Reijden, Joël (2005/2023). Supranational society: masterlist of 2,000 ngos and the top 400 people in them. Institute for the study of globalization and covert politics. https://www.isgp-studies.com/ngo-list-foundations-and-think-tanks-worldwide (accessed: Dec. 2023).

Vogt, Karl Christoph (1859). *Mein Prozeß gegen die Allgemeine Zeitung: Stenographischer Bericht, Dokumente und Erläuterungen*, 166f, 171.

Vossische Zeitung (04.05.1929), 1.

Walden, Jesco (1960). *Und morgen die ganze Welt?: Die Verschwörung der braunen Paladine.* Kongress-Verlag, 25.

Waldner, Wolfgang (2020). *Der preußische Regierungsagent Karl Marx: Wie der Schwager des preußischen Innenministers Ferdinand von Westphalen der berühmte Theoretiker des Sozialismus wurde.* Arnshaugk Verlag, 393f.

Wesel, Uwe (2022). *Geschichte des Rechts: Von den Frühformen bis zur Gegenwart, 5th ed.* C.H. Beck, 182.

Willis, H. Parker (December 1895). Income Taxation in France. *Journal of Political Economy, 4(1)* 37–53(37f).

Winkler, H. A. (2000). *Der lange Weg nach Westen: Deutsche Geschichte vom Ende des Alten Reiches bis zum Untergang der Weimarer Republik.* Germany: Beck, 143.

Wünsche, Horst Friedrich. (2015). *Ludwig Erhards Soziale Marktwirtschaft: Wissenschaftliche Grundlagen und politische Fehldeutungen.* Lau Verlag, 30.

Yergin, Daniel (1990/2009). *The prize: the epic quest for oil, money & power*. Free Press, 770.
ZBW Press Archives (n.d.).
Zitelmann, Rainer (2017). *Hitler:Selbstverständnis eines Revolutionärs*. Lau-Verlag, 325.
Zitelmann, Rainer (2022). *Die 10 Irrtümer der Anti-Kapitalisten: Zur Kritik der Kapitalismuskritik*. Finanzbuchverlag, 214, 340f, 346.

www.ingramcontent.com/pod-product-compliance
Lightning Source LLC
Chambersburg PA
CBHW051255250726
48656CB00004B/1310